Year 8

Changes and Challenges

June Saunders
Christine de Marcellus Vollmer

GRACEWING

First published in Spanish in 2006 by
Alianza Latinoamericana para la Familia en el Perú (ALAFA Perú) as
Vamos hacia la madurez (teacher book seven of the series *Aprendiendo a Querer*)

This English language edition first published in the European Union 2009

Gracewing
2 Southern Avenue, Leominster
Herefordshire, HR6 0QF
United Kingdom
www.gracewing.co.uk

Illustrated by Paul Yanque

ISBN 978 0 85244 718 5

Printed by Athenaeum Press Ltd, Gateshead

Contents

Contents

Books in this Series

Authors:

June Saunders (USA)
Specialist in Marriage and Family Studies and the Ethics of Interpersonal Relations
Co-author of *Cultivating Heart and Character: Educating for Life's Most Essential Goals*
Teacher: Language Arts, Character Education

Christine de Marcellus Vollmer (Venezuela - USA)
President - Alliance for the Family
President - Latin-American Alliance for the Family (ALAFA)
Member - Pontifical Academy for Life
Member - Pontifical Council for the Family
Member - Academic Council for Values Education, University of Carabobo (Venezuela)

Contributors:

Carlos Eduardo Beltramo Álvarez (Argentina)
BA in Philosophy at UPAEP and a member of the Center of Bioethics at UPAEP (Mexico)
Visiting Professor at the University of La Sabana (Colombia) Family Institute, University of San Pablo Family and Marriage Institute (Peru), and the University of La Gran Colombia (Colombia)

The publishers of the English edition of Alive to the World wish to express their deep gratitude to Dominic Marshall for all his comments and advice on the preparation of this text, and to Louise Kirk, Christina Darby, Susan Cooper and Susan Barnes for their unfailing enthusiasm and diligence in its editing.

It is a great pleasure to bring you **Changes and Challenges**, Year 8 of the *Alive to the World* series. This book is the result of years of research by a mixed team of international specialists and is focused on the typical interests, doubts and concerns of students aged 12—13. The topics covered develop themes brought out earlier in the series, but they are now taken a step further.

Changes and Challenges responds to the pre-teenager who is not yet not fully adolescent. This is a transitional time, when new issues found in adolescence conflict with the familiar ones of childhood. It is when young people, beginning to mature, withdraw from the patterns and safety of childhood in order to begin the journey towards adulthood. It is, in general, a pivotal time in the process of growing up.

Twelve-year-olds are faced with many new challenges and choices. We have tried to present in our story the concerns common among them and to explore doubts frequently found in their minds. Throughout the book, you will find that the adventures and interactions of the characters lead the readers to look more closely at concepts which at first appear to conflict—such as freedom and responsibility; belonging to a family, yet growing more independent of it; developing one's own skills while stooping to help the less developed; wanting to stand out, yet being afraid to do so; wanting to belong to the crowd, but also wanting to retain and develop one's own sense of identity and value.

We also consider the effects of hormones which start at this age to cause physical changes and changes to patterns of thought and reaction. The students learn how to handle their own and their peers' developing sexuality with respect and responsibility. Health and hygiene, including grooming and purity of thought, are discussed. Advice is given for coping with the mood swings, frustrations, and the ambivalences of this transitional stage of life.

We believe that this book, through stories about a set of friends and relatives, and brief biographies of some historical figures, will give the students the opportunity to examine a great variety of circumstances and personalities. Our aim is that they should enjoy doing so and become motivated themselves in the process.

I hope you will enjoy this book and find it a useful tool in the vital work of shaping the unique personalities of the maturing young students entrusted to your care.

Christine de Marcellus Vollmer

We wish to thank all the professionals, parents and teenagers who, through their support, experience and advice, have seen Alive to the World *turn from dream to reality.*

Alive to the World—a programme for the effective delivery of PSHE in partnership with parents

Personal, Social and Health Education (PSHE) and Citizenship are subjects which are becoming ever more integral to the curriculum and are recognised as fundamental to the formation and well-being of children today. This is the case in schools not only in the UK but throughout the world.

The role schools can play, in partnership with parents, in engendering good values in young people is now a focus for educational forums at a national level, as is their role in pre-empting antisocial behaviour such as drug and alcohol abuse, bullying, eating disorders, teenage pregnancy and sexually transmitted diseases. *Alive to the World* starts from the premise that it is the young people of strong and well-balanced character who are best equipped to avoid negative behaviour, and that the values which shape good character are universal and can be taught. Training in virtue is seen to be as important to a child's education as forming the mind, in which the role of schools complements that of parents and family, whose prime responsibility the programme respects. *Alive to the World* helps teachers to work in partnership with parents so as to bring out the best in young people, at home, in the school community and in society as a whole.

Alive to the World is a complete **values education programme** which includes Citizenship and Sex and Relationship Education (SRE), and covers all the Government's target topics for PSHE (for further information, please refer to the website **www.alivetotheworld.co.uk**).

Description of the books

Alive to the World consists of a series of twelve books covering ages 6 to 18. The **Student Books** each have 35 chapters, corresponding to the academic year. They contain themed episodes in a single, well illustrated story which follows the lives of two families, their neighbours, friends and teachers as they try to build healthy relationships while sharing life's joys and setbacks. The themes of the stories are further reinforced through brief biographical and historical references. Students will identify with the characters in the story, learning from their experiences and emotions and discovering new modes of good behaviour which will help them in their own lives. Students are encouraged to share the books with their families.

Alive to the World's highly readable stories are carefully gauged to the students' ages. They are based on extensive research by Alliance for the Family (AFF)'s international team of professionals—teachers, psychologists, and social scientists—and the cooperation of large numbers of parents, children and teenagers. Beginning with concepts such as the sense of self, of family, of teamwork (both at school and in the home), of order and of looking out for other people, they explore the physical and emotional development of the growing student. A wide variety of topics is covered within each book, for example making friends, responding to new influences, standing up to peer pressure, becoming alive to sexual attraction and choosing future studies or occupations while looking ahead to marriage and future family life. A **Framework** of topics in the present book is given after this Introduction.

Each Student Book is accompanied by a comprehensive **Teacher Guide** which offers detailed lesson plans and supporting activities. In line with *Alive to the World's* view that character development encompasses the whole person, rather than the intellect only, the approach to learning is threefold:

Knowing—we learn and understand something (through our reason and intelligence).

Accepting—we accept and identify with what we have learned (through the feelings and the will).

Doing—we apply the new knowledge to how we behave (through our actions).

Sexuality and Relationship Education (SRE)

An important and integral part of our human makeup is formed by our sexuality. The *Alive to the World* programme understands sexuality in its fullest sense: we are sexual beings in our biology, our psychology, our spirituality and in how we relate to others socially. It is by learning to understand and respect our sexuality that we become balanced individuals, able to mix freely and successfully and to form the lasting friendships which prepare us for marriage and for bringing up the families of the future.

There are many suggestions given in the chapters of this Guide to help teachers deal with this delicate subject positively and without being judgmental. Wherever possible, parents should be encouraged to discuss aspects of the course, especially Sex and Relationship Education, with their children, and be invited to impart particularly sensitive information themselves. With this in mind, the chapters on the biology of menstruation and conception which accompany Years 6 and 7 have been reserved as computer downloads; they, and the notes which accompany them, can then be printed out and given to parents, or taught at school, as preferred (please see our website **www.alivetotheworld.co.uk**).

Conceptual framework

The course views all aspects of development as integral to the human person. This means that sexuality, as one aspect, is viewed along anthropological principles as a unity of the body and the mind. Each person is regarded as having intrinsic value, with consequent demands in terms of ethics (including sexual) and behaviour.

Alive to the World addresses areas of human development on the four levels of action recommended by the current PSHE syllabus:

Biological—identity, modesty, health, self-control and skills.

Psychological—psychosexual development of the personality, self knowledge, self-esteem, assertiveness and good habits.

Spiritual—(the intelligence and the will)—openness to spiritual development; intellectual and moral maturity.

Social—maturity in relationships with family, friends, community and in marriage.

The books divide into two overall stages of development: childhood (Years 2—8); and adolescence (Years 9—13).

A flexible programme

The material in the Student Books can be used in a variety of ways. If curriculum time is short, the stories are easy to read and can be prepared by students in advance of the class when specific issues can be explored further.

The programme has been used successfully with groups both large and small. The important thing is to create an environment in which students feel free to share their thoughts. The activities in the Student Book and Teacher Guide are well suited or easily adapted for circle time and for using other teaching methods in which sharing is encouraged.

Material within the Guide could also be used as a basis for workshops with parents or guardians where appropriate.

Accompanying computer programs

Interactive computer programs are currently being developed to help with lesson preparation and extend *Alive to the World's* range. Please see our website at **www.alivetotheworld.co.uk** for further information.

A   GENERAL FRAMEWORK

Set out below, with an index to follow, is the framework of topics addressed in Year 8. You may find this useful in creating your lesson plans.

Specific Objectives

UNIT	SUBJECT	CHAPTERS
I. Building My Freedom	The responsibility which comes from growing freedom is explained; also the need for discipline and self-control.	1, 2, 3, 4, 5
II. My Personality	Personal dignity, and esteem for self and others, are emphasised as students undergo physical and emotional changes; also countering new issues in peer pressure.	6, 7, 8, 9, 10, 11
III. My Family and My Future	Some family relationships are described, including family as our first and trusted friends, the role of each member in resolving conflicts, the proper use of authority, and respect due to the elderly.	12, 13, 14
IV. Relationships	Friendships outside the family are of growing importance during adolescence. Developing the capacity for loyal friendship prepares the student for even more lasting commitments in later life, especially for marriage. Relations with members of the opposite sex are explored, together with dating, its purpose and why embarking on it prematurely causes problems. Relationships within the family continue to be studied, together with the importance of thinking ahead to a future career.	15, 16, 17, 18, 19, 20, 21, 22
V. Changes in My Life—Puberty	The changes that the student goes through in adolescence have repercussions in all areas of life: physical, psychological, social and spiritual. These various changes are explained, together with the need to exercise patience with self and with others, to control mood swings, to listen and communicate clearly, and to understand and respect a growing right to privacy.	23, 24, 25, 26, 27, 28, 29, 30
VI. My Health	Health (mental, spiritual and physical) are increasingly the student's own responsibility. The dangers of pornography and masturbation are described, as are those of smoking and drug-taking. The importance to general well-being of exercise, hygiene, diet and sleep is emphasised	31, 32, 33, 34, 35

B   STUDENT WORKBOOK INDEX

Unit III: My Family and My Future

12.	Family Life and Strife	To respect and value the family	Maturation in group dynamics: the family
13.	Who's In Charge?	Respect for legitimate authority	Group maturity
14.	The 'Generation Gap'	Respect for experience and elders	Group maturity

Unit IV: Relationships

15.	Romeo and Juliet?	Friendship	Group maturity: friendship Group maturity: the couple
16.	Charts and Chilli Peppers	Dating	Group maturity: the couple
17.	To Live Happily Ever After	Marriage	Group maturity: the couple
18.	The Power of One	Virtues needed in a happy family	Group maturity: in the family
19.	Dad's Promise	Relationships within the family	Development of virtues Family dynamics
20	The Family	The family in society and history	Group maturity: family and society
21	Faithful Friend	Fidelity as the basis of all friendships	Developing the character strength (virtue) of fidelity
22	Dreams and Schemes: Looking at the Future	Visualizing the future with idealism and realism	Seeing in perspective Goal-setting

Unit V: Changes in my Life (Puberty)

23	Going through Changes	Respecting the changes that puberty brings	Initial stages of puberty
24	Privacy, Please!	Respecting privacy	The self among others
25	Invasion of Privacy	Respecting the opposite sex	Setting personal boundaries
26	'Cousins' Talk	Hormonal changes of puberty and their influence	Coping with transition
27	Stones on the Path	The changing moods of puberty well-being	Taking responsibility for one's own well-being and that of others
28	Now!!	Impatience and frustration	Developing the virtue of patience Seeing in perspective
29	Learning Your Limits—Soothing Irritability	Irritability	Healthy habits Self-regulation
30	Communication	Communication and its advantages	Decisiveness and self-control

Unit VI: My Health

32	'Blondie'	Pornography	Responsibility for self and others: self-control and social awareness
33	Solitary 'Pleasures'	Masturbation	Self-control Preparation for intimacy rather than isolation
34	Rebel with a Cause	The importance of sports in maintaining health of body and mind	Responsibility Self-respect
35	*Mens Sana in Corpore Sano*	A healthy mind in a healthy body	Self-care Positive outlook

Introductory Class

Objectives

- ▶ Establish rapport with students.
- ▶ Introduce the scope of the subject.
- ▶ Explain the topics and how they are covered.
- ▶ Discover the students' interests and current knowledge.
- ▶ Become aware of their concerns.

General Information

How you give the Introductory Class will depend on the rapport which already exists between teacher and students. A teacher who has already taught the *Alive to the World* programme to the same class in an earlier year will be in a very different position from a teacher with students fresh to the programme. Though the content of the Introductory Class will vary, its aim is to win the confidence of the students and make sure that those who are new to the school feel as much part of the programme as their classmates. It should offer an overview of the coming year and bring out any particular interests or sensitivities.

Towards the end of the books, the subject matter becomes more intimate (see especially Units IV to VI—*Relationships, Changes in My Life and My Health*). Students may notice this as you go through the topics with them. Additional material, for instance on Sexually Transmitted Diseases, is being made available for download from our website (www.allianceforfamily.org), and you may want to intersperse this with the topics given in the books. It is warmly recommended that you become familiar in good time with what is available, and that you refer to the website periodically for the latest information.

Class plan

Explain that *Alive to the World* is different from other courses on the academic curriculum. Students will be learning some important facts but they will also be expanding their horizons with truths based on common sense, which they will be encouraged to adopt and implement in their own lives. The lessons should be fun, and students will get most out of them if they are honest in their opinions and respectful of those of others. Exchanges which are personal should be contained within the classroom and not talked about outside. This is important in establishing an atmosphere of confidence in which pupils can talk and interact openly.

Immediately before this Chapter, you will find a Framework of the topics to be covered together with an Index of subjects (pp. 14—17). Use these to give the students an overview of what they can expect in the year ahead. Ask them to open the Index of their Student Books and run through with them the unit and chapter headings. Then give them an overview of the book, explaining that they will be learning by following the story of a group of school-children of their own age. Encourage them to take the books home and show them to their parents.

Activity 1

Write on the board or display on screen a list of the main topics which will be covered. Ask the students to pick out and rank from 1—6:

(a)   the 6 topics that they think will be of most use to them;

(b)   the 6 topics that they most look forward to studying.

Find out from the students which topics from (a) and (b) rank the highest. This exercise will help students to focus on what lies ahead for them, and give you a feel for their particular concerns and interests.

Activity 2

Divide the class into groups and ask them to come up with their own rules for the class, such as not laughing at other people's comments, not shouting someone else down, not talking externally about what goes on in class, not being forced to talk. Invite a spokesman for each group to come up with the group's ideas. Write on the board the rules which the class as a whole wishes to adopt. Think about sanctions should someone break the rules.

Get the class to copy down the rules, or circulate copies at the next lesson.

**Unit I:
Building My Freedom**

Abilities:
* To understand that growing freedom brings increasing responsibility;
* To value self-discipline and strength of character;
* To see that these are essential in becoming free and responsible adults.
Number of Chapters: 5 (1 to 5).

Chapter 1
I Don't Want to Grow up! Freedom and Responsibility

General Information

Topic

Freedom and responsibility.

Content

▸ Addressing ambivalence about the growing up process.
▸ The interrelationship of freedom and responsibility.
▸ Definition of responsibility and its role in fulfilling relationships and personal happiness.

Objectives

Knowing
▸ To relate freedom and responsibility to growing up in a positive way.
▸ Understanding the connection between maturity, responsibility, and good relationships.

Accepting
▸ To want to grow more responsible and free.
▸ To be interested in new rights and obligations.
▸ To accept responsibility as promoting happiness in relationships.

Doing
▸ To identify ways to attain new rights and better relationships through fulfilling obligations and to try to incorporate them in real life.

Areas of Human Development to be Emphasised

▶ Learning and self-management.

▶ Relating responsibility to happiness and fulfilment.

▶ Growth in freedom and responsibility.

Procedural Suggestions

It is essential that students realise the importance of reading each chapter in advance and reaching their own conclusions. Encourage them to present questions to be discussed in class.

Class Plan

1   Knowing

Motivation

Start an informal dialogue with students on their opinions of the Chapter. Choose one or two students to summarise its content. Ask if any of the students could identify with Charlie or Alice—or if any of them has ever wanted all freedom and no responsibility?

Story context:

This chapter introduces some of the main young characters: Charlie and his cousin, Alice. Having seen a play version of Peter Pan, Charlie realises that he is growing up but that, like Peter Pan, he doesn't want to because of the responsibility involved.

He wants to be 'free'. Alice, his mother and his teacher challenge his ideas of responsibility and freedom.

Introduction

Charlie, reluctant at first to assume more adult responsibility, is encouraged to empathise and respond appropriately to his mother's needs.

Presentation

Key Ideas

▶ Sometimes children experience conflicting feelings about growing up, wanting to stay 'free' of responsibilities.

▶ Freedom and responsibility are complementary and inseparable.

▶ Responsibility need not be onerous. Defined as 'response-ability' it means responding joyfully to others' needs and situations; it is the courage to face the results of our actions, and the key to happiness, growth, and good relationships.

Topic Development

A   Ambivalence about growing up

Misconceptions about freedom and responsibility sometimes keep children (and adults!) from wanting to be mature. They want to be 'free' and to avoid responsibilities. Ask students how many of them have ever felt they didn't want to grow up.

To counter this ambivalence ask students to do Activity 2 of Accepting–Guided Work.

Usually the 'Pros' will involve more freedom than the students now have, while the 'Cons' will involve the responsibilities of being an adult. Most students will probably find more 'Pros' than 'Cons', as they have a natural inclination toward maturity.

First conclusion: Freedom and responsibility are part of being grown up.

B   The interrelationship of Freedom and Responsibility

Freedom and responsibility are actually closely related. If we are not responsible, we lose some freedom. The examples from the story are irresponsible eating leading to overweight and loss of mobility; disobedience of traffic laws leading to jams, etc. Later chapters show that sexual 'freedom' without responsibility leads to diseases and damaged relationships. To be free from these we must also accept responsibility.

Ask students for other examples that behaving irresponsibly means losing freedom (committing a crime and going to jail is one obvious example).

C   Definition of Responsibility as 'Response-Ability to the Needs of Others'

Redefining responsibility as responding to the needs of others takes some of the onus out of it— 'Response-ability'. On the board write 'Responsibility = Response-ability'. Explain that this *great ability* is related to happiness and love. Maturity involves learning how to give so as to benefit and enhance another's well-being. This is true love, and brings joy. Point out that Charlie learns that his parents undertake responsibilities out of love for him and his siblings—to serve their needs. He also learns that by responding to the needs of his mother he experiences happiness.

D   Second conclusion:

Responsibility is to be welcomed as an integral part of freedom, love, and happiness.

2   Accepting

Guided Work

Activity 1

Ask students to imagine that they are in 'Never Land' and will stay children forever. However, they have been 'frozen' at age two. They must still wear nappies, they have difficulty talking, can't read, write, dress themselves, etc. Are they happy to be permanently so?

Activity 2

Ask students to divide a sheet of paper into two columns. On the left side ask them to write 'Pros', and on the right 'Cons', and to list the Pros and Cons of being grown-up.

Pros might be: being able to drive, have money, to be in charge, etc.

Cons might be: paying bills, taxes, rent, etc.

Activity 3

Ask students to make a list of chores they could do at home to free up some time for their parents. Ask them to do one of those chores each day for a week, and then evaluate how this action changed their relationship with their parents.

Activity 4

Tell students to look at Activity 1 in their Student Books (p.218).

Activity 1

> Make a list of some things you couldn't do last year but you can do now because you are older.
>
> Have your parents given you new privileges or responsibilities?
>
> Are you allowed to do some things now that you couldn't do before? Go to more places on your own or with friends?
>
> Do you get more pocket money, or perhaps earn money for the first time?
>
> Are you better at a sport, or a hobby or an activity?
>
> Has your handwriting or artistic ability improved?

Ask students what are the responsibilities needed for these privileges. Find out whether they accept the responsibilities linked to the privileges (e.g., can they go to the park with friends, *and* be responsible enough to report back home by a certain time?)

3   Doing

Evaluation

Activity 1

Ask students to pool ideas about being stuck at a certain developmental stage. What are the most negative and uncomfortable aspects?

Activity 2

Write the pros and cons of being a grown-up on the board, emphasising the positive.

Point out that they may perceive some things as cons since they lack a mature adult's tools to face those problems; however, they may change their view as they grow up.

Activity 3

During the following week assess students' commitment to free up some time for their parents. Without being too comprehensive try to show the most positive aspects of the students' experiences.

Activity 4

Together, analyse the general progress students have made so far this year.

Clearly explain the relationship between growth and responsibilities. Emphasise the positive aspect of this growth.

Students should show evidence that significant advances have been made in understanding responsibility's relationship to freedom, growth, and happiness.

Responsibility, freedom, growth and happiness feature throughout the book and underpin the important concepts of sexual responsibility introduced at the end of the book and continued in Year 9.

Specific Resolutions

Ask students to make a list of things they could do to help around the house to give their parents more free time.

Help them resolve to do at least one of these per day, and after a week record the improvements in relationships with parents.

Record any new privileges or freedoms granted for showing responsibility like this.

Chapter 2
Watch Out! Alice Gains Some Independence

General Information

Topic

Autonomy with responsibility.

Content

▸ Gaining autonomy.

▸ The effects of irresponsibility on autonomy and independence.

▸ Accepting adult guidance and help.

Objectives

Knowing

▸ To understand that autonomy, while desirable, requires responsibility and accountability.

▸ To understand that irresponsibility can bring undesirable consequences.

▸ To understand that freedom grows in proportion to proven trustworthiness.

Accepting

▸ To want autonomy and to be willing to show the responsibility it requires.

▸ To trust known responsible adults for guidance, showing interest and concern, and granting freedom as appropriate.

Doing

▸ To find areas in life where greater responsibility may lead to greater autonomy, to accept those responsibilities and their rewards.

Areas of Human Development to be Emphasised

- ▸ Autonomy involves responsibility.
- ▸ Independence is earned through trustworthiness.
- ▸ Managing independence and responsibility under adult guidance.

Class Plan

1   Knowing

Motivation

Briefly discuss the Chapter. Ensure the students have taken it in by asking questions such as: What was Charlie's new responsibility? What was Alice's? Did Alice undertake her responsibility well? What were the consequences of her not doing so? Were the grown-ups in her life helpful to her?

Story context:

Charlie now has the job he wanted in Chapter 1, but this leaves his younger siblings unattended. Alice agrees to babysit, but in consequence skips homework and daydreams. Seeing the results of bad grades and parental anger, she admits her mistakes, accepts guidance from parents and teachers, and becomes more responsible, enjoying the rewards of their renewed trust in her.

Introduction

While all want more independence and autonomy, handling this well can be hard.

Presentation

Key Ideas

- ▸ Autonomy is naturally desirable.
- ▸ Handling it poorly has consequences.
- ▸ Adults can help balance autonomy and freedom, and hold children accountable.
- ▸ Greater trustworthiness leads to greater freedom.

Topic Development

A   Gaining Autonomy

Discuss the chapter with students. In what ways do they wish for more independence? (Students usually have many ideas of this!) In what areas do they wish they could make more of their own decisions? Can they identify with Charlie's wanting to help his family? Can they identify with Alice's enjoying being in charge in her aunt's home, having a key of her own, and dreaming about what to buy with the money she earned?

B   Effects of Irresponsibility on Autonomy and Independence

Ask what sort of responsibilities students have in their daily lives. (Examples: bathing themselves, dressing themselves, having books and schoolbags ready, homework, being polite, perhaps travelling to and from school, household chores, watching siblings, etc.) Do all of these responsibilities lead to greater freedom, trust, and self-confidence? What happens if they don't fulfil these responsibilities?

Ask students to share ideas about what would happen.

C **Accepting Adult Guidance and Help**

Often more privileges are given in return for something to earn them. Do students receive allowances given only in return for certain chores; or rewards for good grades?

c.1. Being Held Accountable by Adults

While being held accountable may seem boring or a hindrance, it helps children develop good habits for life. Alice began to develop the habit of watching time so that she could complete her studies successfully. Her bad habits of daydreaming and skipping homework brought bad consequences.

Ask students to consider the following (from Activity 2A in their Student Books, p.218):

Activity 2 A

Read and think about this:

'Habit'

I am your constant companion. I am your greatest helper or heaviest burden.

I will push you onwards or drag you down to failure. I am completely at your command. Half the things you do you might just as well leave to me and I will be able to do them quickly and correctly.

I am easily managed—all you have to do is be firm with me. Show me exactly how you want something done and after a little practice I will do it for you. I am the servant of all great men; and alas, of all failures, as well. Those who are great, I have made great. Those who are failures, I have made failures.

I am not a machine, though I work with great precision and have the intelligence of a man. You may use me for a profit or run me for ruin—it makes no difference to me.

Take me, train me, be firm with me, and I will place the world at your feet. Be easy on me and I will destroy you. WHO AM I? I AM HABIT!

Anonymous

Accountability trains us to form good habits.

c.2. Adult Helpers

With their wisdom and experience adults can help children know when they have 'bitten off more than they can chew'. They can also guide them toward wise choices and grant them new and appropriate freedoms.

Ask students to discuss the roles of adults in the story and the supplement about the student and the famous professor. Was this adult trustworthy and helpful? When are good times to seek adult help in fulfilling our responsibilities?

2   Accepting

Guided Work

Activity 1

Ask the class, in groups of 3 or 4, to look at Activity 2B in their Student Books (p.219).

Activity 2 B

> 1.   Part of taking responsibility is working out how much you can and can't do in a given amount of time. Have you ever 'bitten off more than you could chew'? (Even grown-ups do this sometimes.)
>
> 2.   Why was Alice uncomfortable about having to go to adults (her teacher and her aunt) and admit that she was doing more than she could do well? Were the adults kind to her?
>
> 3.   Was Alice's decision about how to spend the money she'd earned a wise one?
>
> 4.   Did you think Alice's parents were too easy on her when her grades went down? Were they too harsh? Or just about right?
>
> 5.   Was the student uncomfortable asking the famous Professor Van Allen to let her drop out of his course? Was he kind to her?

Activity 2

Read the story of Alfred the Great and burning the cakes. It is on pp 196-198 in William Bennett's *The Book of Virtues* (widely available on the internet or through booksellers). Or use the following synopsis in Activity 2C (Student Book, p.219):

Activity 2 C–King Alfred the Great

> Read and find out more about Alfred the Great.
>
> King Alfred is considered one of the greatest kings ever, earning the epithet 'the Great'. When the Danes were attacking England, though, he suffered great defeats. His army scattered, and he himself escaped to an island to hide. He sought shelter in a farmer's cottage. The farmer was not home, but the wife agreed to give him dinner if he would watch the 'cakes' on the stove while she went outside briefly. (These are likely to have been something like pancakes, cooked directly on the hob.) While watching the cakes, Alfred became absorbed in his worries about the kingdom. Soon the cakes started burning, and the cottage filled full of smoke. The farmer's wife came in, shouting and scolding. Then the farmer came in and recognised the King. He told his wife to stop scolding the King, but the King said she was right to do so—he had said he would watch the cakes and had failed to carry out his responsibility. No responsibility was too small to ignore. King Alfred went on to win many battles and the respect of future generations.

> The moral of this story is that no responsibility, once undertaken, is too insignificant to ignore. The person who is faithful in small things will be faithful in large things too. King Alfred's acceptance of the farmer's wife's scolding shows that he believed in this too. That was probably part of his greatness.

Point out that a friend who can't be trusted with one dollar certainly can't be trusted with a hundred. The better someone is at keeping faith with small responsibilities, the more trustworthy with larger ones. Now is the time for the students to practise being faithful in their small responsibilities so as to develop the character strengths needed to be faithful in life's big responsibilities—marriage, family, career, finances, citizenship, etc.

3   Doing

Evaluation

Activity 1

Ask the groups to share their ideas, experiences, and opinions and compare them with those of the characters in the story.

Specific Resolutions

To choose a specific privilege or mark of independence wished for during the idea-sharing session.

To resolve to discuss with parents or other responsible adults what the student must do to earn and keep that privilege.

To strive toward gaining that privilege and living up to its attendant responsibilities.

Chapter 3
He is Mighty who Conquers Himself

General Information

Topic

Strength and self-discipline.

Contents

▶ Strength, properly understood, is mental as well as physical.

▶ Self-control and self-discipline.

▶ Strength in relationship to others.

Objectives

Knowing

▶ To discover and understand that strength and self-discipline are necessary for maturity.

▶ To understand that 'being one's own master' means that being truly in command of oneself requires self-discipline.

▶ To value inner strength as well as physical strength.

Accepting

▶ To become interested in being strong and self-disciplined.

▶ To realise the importance of strengthening both mind and body.

Doing

▶ To see how strength and discipline can apply in daily life.

Areas of Human Development to be Emphasised

▶ Body-spirit integration.

▶ Self-control and self-discipline.

▶ Responsibility in relationships.

Class Plan

1 Knowing

Motivation

Ask students some questions: whether they want to become 'strong'; which 'strong' people they admire; what kind of strengths these people display.

Story context:

Charlie is interested in becoming 'strong'. His coach teaches him about the inner strength of self-control and self-discipline; he challenges him to live up to this.

Introduction

Strength of mind as well as body is true strength, and commands the respect of others.

Presentation

Key Ideas

- Strength is not just physical, but includes self-discipline and self-control.
- Conquering one's destructive impulses is the greatest strength
- Such strength commands respect and improves relationships

Topic Development

A Definition of strength as mental as well as physical

Emphasise that defining strength as physical strength alone is inadequate, ignoring the moral and mental strength needed to do well in life. Charlie yearns to be 'strong' like a professional footballer. He is thinking only in terms of muscle strength. His coach tells him that real strength is that of character; it involves saying no to oneself, and using judgment and discernment so as not to give in every impulse and desire that occurs.

References to saying no to drugs, or holding back from doing too much at once (Charlie was forcing himself to do too many push-ups) should be emphasised as examples of the 'other' kind of strength.

Mr Jackson tells Charlie of the saying: 'He is mighty who conquers himself'. He says that doing this shows real strength. It includes things like being true to family and friends even when people are mocking them and working when we don't want to.

B Self-control and self-discipline

This chapter emphasises that restraint when one is angered and/or hurt takes strength too—maybe the greatest strength. Charlie loses control of himself when Malik teases him, and he shoves Malik hard. Rebuking him, Mr Jackson, for an example to Charlie of self-control, relates how Dr. Martin Luther King did not retaliate when whites bombed his home and nearly hurt his wife and baby.

"The whole world changed a little bit for the better because Dr. King refused to strike back. That's real strength—in fact, so much strength it changed history."

Even though Malik provoked Charlie's retaliation, Mr Jackson asserts that Charlie should have had the self-discipline not to strike back.

C   Responsibility in Relationships

Another aspect of inner strength is the willingness to show responsibility in human relationships. On the positive side it means taking initiative in the relationship, sharing expenses, being willing to be first to invite the other home, etc. In a negative sense, it means taking responsibility for personal faults, flaws, and mistakes which affect the relationship. Charlie makes himself apologise to Malik, taking responsibility for his part in their quarrel. This requires great effort for Charlie. Far from thinking Charlie a 'wimp' for doing this, Malik admits his own fault, accepts a handshake, and expresses respect in front of others for Charlie's 'strength'—both inner and outer.

2   Accepting

Guided Work

Activity 1

Part A

All of us, especially boys, have firm ideas of what 'strength' is, what being 'tough' is, and what not being a 'wimp' means.

Ask the students to read Activity 3A (p.220 of their Student Books) about the karate instructor. Break them into small groups to discuss the karate instructor's remark: "The hardest thing I ever did was walk away from a fight." Ask them to answer the questions in their discussions.

Activity 3 A

> What do you think?
>
> A karate instructor who was a twelfth-degree black belt once told his students, "The hardest thing I ever did was walk away from a fight." He had grown up in a tough neighbourhood and had been fighting all his life. When he discovered karate, he realised that fighting should only be for self-defence. The tough guys from his neighbourhood did not realise that, though! What do you suppose they thought of him when he wouldn't fight? Would they have thought him a 'wimp'? What kind of strength does it take not to fight?

Part B

For balance, ask students to name times when a person should use force—for instance, self-defence against a serious attacker, defending someone weaker, police capturing criminals, to defend one's country, etc.

Discuss legitimate uses of force, emphasising that most common interactions among people do not call for its use.

Activity 2 Developing inner strength

Ask students to look at and try Activity 3B, featured in the student book.

What kind of strength do they think doing this might take? Would it be easier to do ten push-ups or to do this?

Activity 3 B

Try saying only nice things for just one hour—nothing sarcastic or complaining, or critical of someone else. Is it easy or difficult? If it was easy, try it for two hours or a whole day. You might want to write a small report about this or make an entry in your journal.

Activity 3

Ask students to think about an 'everyday hero' who shows strength in daily life. It might be a parent who, after working hard all day, comes home and helps the children with their homework. It might be a local person who voluntarily gives up time to help others, in spite of being just as busy as everyone else.

Ask them to write a letter of appreciation to this person for showing an example of quiet strength.

3 Doing

Evaluation

Activity 1

Encourage each group to present its conclusions in class.

Part A

Emphasise that strength should not be understood in a merely physical sense. Real strength is shown by those who do not resort to using physical violence.

Part B

Explain that sometimes we must apply a certain degree of physical strength to reach certain goals. Students must understand that this must be done with caution and only as a last resort.

Specific Resolutions

To develop strength of character as well as outer strength or physical accomplishments.

To determine to show 'real strength' in fulfilling obligations: being true to one's word, living up to responsibilities at home and at school, even when one doesn't want to.

To take responsibility for one's own part in conflicts, regardless of the other person's actions or attitude.

Chapter 4
Speech! Speech!
Charlie Deals with Fear

 General Information

Topic

The wish for freedom and accomplishment versus lack of self-confidence.

Content

- Fears are common, but they can limit us.
- With help and guidance, we can face our fears and conquer them.
- The sense of victory is wonderful, and it can carry over to new challenges.

Objectives

Knowing
- To understand how the wish for freedom and accomplishment can be hampered by lack of confidence at this age.

Accepting
- To realise the need for patience and courage in gaining self-confidence.

Doing
- To recognise situations in daily life where lack of confidence hampers growth toward freedom and accomplishment.
- To know how to cope with this.

Areas of Human Development to be Emphasised

- Achievement over inferiority.
- Coping strategies.
- Self-confidence.

Class Plan

1   Knowing

Motivation

Ask students whether fear or lack of self-confidence ever holds them back from doing something they would really like to do.

Story context:

Charlie wants to enter a contest and win the big prize but his fear of public speaking threatens to hold him back. Finally, he faces his fear, learns coping skills, and goes on to victory.

Introduction

Facing fears, with wisdom and guidance, can lead to welcome, unexpected triumphs. Charlie triumphs over his fear, giving a superb performance. He the feels elated.

Presentation

Key Ideas

> Fears are common.

> Fears can interfere with achieving what we really want.

> There are ways to face fears, often with adult help, so that we can achieve victory and grow in confidence and accomplishments.

Topic Development

Victory brings euphoria and can also lead to new challenges.

A   Fears are common, but they can limit us

Charlie's teacher said that, according to surveys, the two things human beings fear most are: death and public speaking! "So you're not alone," she tells Charlie.

Further, the symptoms of 'stage fright' are well-known and extremely common: The physical symptoms include: *sweating palms, 'butterflies' in the stomach, a dry throat, a thumping heart. She said that nerves showed that you wanted to do a good job and that they could help you prepare better beforehand.*

Mrs Alam also told him that many famous people get nervous every time they sing or act, no matter how many times they have done it before. She talked about William Faulkner, who won the Nobel Prize for Literature. He was a great writer, but he was scared to death of giving the Acceptance Speech in front of all the dignitaries from around the world. She produced a picture of Faulkner. He looked shy, like Charlie.

Some famous singers or actors have confessed to being afraid every time before going on stage. It's normal and natural to experience some 'nerves' in these and other situations where we want to do well.

We should not let our fears prevent us from achieving our goals. Charlie, even though *a wave of fear spread over him,* felt a real desire to win—*to prove himself in public.*

In the end, the contest is a very memorable experience for Charlie. He has the added bonus of being asked to become a student correspondent for the newspaper. This will boost his future career prospects and give him pride and self-confidence in the present.

B   With help and guidance, we can conquer our fears

Charlie has the support and help of his teacher, who coaches him, and his parents, his cousin, and his aunt and uncle:

But then he saw his mum looking at him with such confidence and love that he realised how much he wanted her and Dad to be proud of him. And the others, he thought—his whole family was there, and Alice's too.

He heard Mum whisper, "I hope you win, dear. But, if you don't, you can be proud that you came this far."

…Mum said, "That was excellent, Charlie." Dad was still clapping. Alice just giggled with excitement.

"You've got to have won!" she whispered frantically.

"We'll see," said Mum. "Anyway, he's already won. Just being here and doing such a good job is a victory."

With the support of others, we can conquer our fear. It is important not to try to 'go it alone'. That's what friends, teachers, and parents are for!

C   Victory brings elation, and can also lead to new challenges

Charlie feels elated after he has delivered his speech:

Charlie's mind was whirling. He had done it—he had conquered his fear.

Everyone thinks that he 'won' the contest even though he came second. There are wonderful rewards. Charlie is complimented by one of the judges, who invites him to write a student article for the newspaper once a month:

She said, "Charlie, I just wanted to tell you that I thought your essay and your reading of it were terrific."

His teacher expresses admiration: *"You did so well… I never saw anyone work so hard to conquer his nerves."*

Charlie now has the confidence to take on new challenges. When his teacher tells him of a forthcoming debate, he feels *a rush of confidence.*

Consciously remembering times we have been triumphant can give us confidence for embarking on new challenging situations.

2   Accepting

Guided Work

Activity 1

Ask students to read Activity 4 in their student book (p.226) and answer the questions.

Activity 4

> Some fears are natural—fear of being in an accident, fear of getting hurt, getting ill, losing someone you love. Others are more in our minds—getting up to speak in public, for instance.
>
> What are some of your fears?
>
> How do you handle them?

Do you feel that an adult might help you face up to your fears with wise advice and encouragement?

Do you go to such adults when you are frightened?

Activity 2

Tell students that relaxation and fear cannot co-exist. Ask them to try these exercises:

▸ Take twenty long, deep breaths, then to note how relaxed they feel.

▸ Tense their fists for 10 seconds, then to relax their fists and notice the relaxed feelings, repeating to themselves, "This is how it feels to relax from tension."

▸ Imagine themselves in a warm and completely safe and relaxing environment: in front of the TV at home with no pressures on; in a warm bathtub full of soapy water and bath oil; at the beach on a perfect day; as a kitten asleep nestled in its mother's fur; or any of their own personal places of relaxation.

Ask them to note how relaxed they are after imagining these things. Tell them they can use these techniques in any challenging situation: before a difficult conversation or phone call, before having to make a speech, before a trying social situation, or a test.

These are proven techniques. The idea is to impress upon the students that they can relax and lose tension, thus gaining more confidence to face challenging situations.

Activity 3

Ask the students to discuss in small groups times they have been afraid to do something and yet have overcome their fear and triumphed.

3   Doing

Evaluation

Activity 1

Discuss student book Activity 4 with the class. Try to present many strategies to help them face their fears. Students may be reluctant to participate at first, but should loosen up later in the activity. Encourage their participation. Try to draw conclusions that will help them in their efforts to overcome their fears.

Activity 2

Encourage groups actively to include everybody in the discussion and contributions.

Try to create a positive atmosphere in class, allowing every student to find the tools needed to overcome fear and their possible reluctance to join in.

Specific Resolution

The next time a challenge requiring self-confidence appears, to take it up, using the help, support and guidance of adults, the ideas in this story, and maybe some of the relaxation exercises.

Chapter 5
Flying High and Swooping Down

General Information

Topic

Personal benefit and benefit of the wider group..

Content

- ▶ The paradox of the whole.
- ▶ Lesson from nature: the 'V' Formation.
- ▶ Caring selflessly for others.

Objectives

Knowing
- ▶ To understand the difference between what is good for self and what is good for all. To learn to recognise when the two are in conflict.

Accepting
- ▶ To value acting for the common good: it also brings personal fulfilment.

Doing
- ▶ To discern personal interest and common good in specific situations.

Areas of Human Development to be Emphasised

- ▶ Seeing in perspective.
- ▶ Self-growth in relation to others.
- ▶ Community awareness.

Class Plan

1 Knowing

Motivation

Discuss the strength of working together. Demonstrate with craft or cocktail sticks. Alone, each stick easily breaks, but together even a few sticks are impossible to snap.

Story context:

The skilled Year 8 pupils must learn to share their gym period with the unskilled Year 6.

Introduction

Sharing and caring.

Presentation

Key Ideas

▸ By helping others we also help ourselves.

▸ Cooperation creates new strengths.

Topic Development

A   The Paradox of the Whole

A paradox is something that appears impossible, and yet is true. Paradoxically, by helping others we ourselves are helped. When Charlie and the Year 8s complain that they cannot advance their own skills while hampered by the Year 6s, the teacher explains the paradox that *"the best way to learn something is to teach it to others. If you lads make an effort to teach the younger ones, your own game will improve."*

Charlie finds this paradox to be true when he helps the Year 6 pupil Calum: *Soon the older boys noticed that their own skills were getting sharper and more accurate too.*

The 'Food for Thought' story in the student book (p.37) is paradoxical:

'Food for Thought'

An old story tells of a man coming upon a group of people in a village high up in the mountains. In this village, the only tools people had to eat with were hugely long forks. The forks were so long that they were difficult to manoeuvre so people went hungry even though there was plenty of food. They hit each other all the time with their elbows, and they found that their arms did not stretch far enough to allow the tips of the forks to reach their mouths.

The visitor looked surprised. "Why don't you simply feed each other?" he suggested. Suddenly no-one needed to go hungry any more!

In spite of plentiful food the people were starving. Paradoxically, when they helped one another and stopped desperately trying to feed themselves all had their fill. Numbers of people, food and forks were the same. Yet by working together they used what was available much more effectively, seeming to multiply the amount of food that they had.

This process is called 'synergy': when 1 + 1 = 3. The saying, 'The whole is greater than the sum of its parts' likewise shows that by cooperative effort people create something greater, more effective and successful than would be possible just by the sum of their individual works.

B   Example from Nature: the 'V' Formation

Nature often gives us examples of tried and true principles of existence. Geese can achieve more as a cooperative group than they would as individuals. Charlie reminds the coach of how he taught them about the "V" formation geese use to fly south:

"You were trying to teach us about teamwork. You told us how geese always fly south in the formation of a V— you said scientists have found out that it's sensible of the geese because flying in a V is less of a strain on their hearts. They found they could glide more and save energy that way. You told us about aerodynamics— that the V was an aerodynamic way to reduce wind resistance. You said the geese could fly 70% further by flying together in a V instead of alone. And they swap over being the head of the V, so no-one gets too tired. You said that was why we should pass and set up shots instead of trying to take all the glory by shooting all the time—to work as a team."

C   Caring Selflessly for Others

It can be self-defeating to help others just to benefit oneself. This is still using others and not really putting the interests of others—of the whole group—first. Although Charlie starts by helping the Year 6 boys in the hope that games will be more fun for Year 8, he and the other Year 8s come to like and appreciate the Year 6s. Charlie notices and begins to help Calum:

Then Charlie noticed one of the younger boys—Calum. He had hair that fell right over his huge, dark eyes. His arms were so skinny, Charlie wondered how he could even throw the ball. What he liked about Calum, though, was that he always tried, no matter what. Even when the older boys laughed at him, he'd just grin, shake his head, and try again.

Charlie started to help Calum. He would tell him something about moving his feet or lining up a shot. Soon he found Calum looking up to him as if he were his hero… Whenever Calum saw Charlie around school, he'd point him out to whoever he was with.

"That's Charlie," he'd say. "He's so cool—and kind."

Charlie and the other older boys feel pride when their Year 6s do something right. And when the Year 8s are pitted against the Year 9s, the juniors provide needed support:

The Year 6 boys decided to come and cheer them on. Being cheered makes a big difference to a team. When Charlie heard Calum shouting them on as though his lungs would burst he tried even harder to win—for him. Each team member gave everything he had—and they won! Delighted, the Year 6s rushed onto court.

The story the Coach tells Charlie of the geese coming down from the sky to help a sick or dying goose is an example of selfless caring:

"When a goose in a flock is sick or dying, two other geese fly with it down to the ground. They stay with the sick goose so it's never alone. It's quite possible that two strong geese might want to be doing something else, isn't it? But they don't. They stay to help, so that no member of the flock is left alone when it's weak. They take care of the goose until it either gets well or dies. Then they either rejoin the flock or go on to form a new one.

The [present Year 6] was not unlike you were a few years ago: unsure of themselves, and needing to be given a boost. What better than to ask them up here and get some stronger geese—to help them!

2 Accepting

Guided Work

Activity 1

Ask the students to write a one-paragraph essay on this topic.

Activity 2

Ask students for a (written) response to Activity 5 in their Student Books (p.221):

Activity 5

> Charlie had to sacrifice his own personal success for the good of others. Have you ever had a personal goal that seemed at odds with something you were asked to do for others—the needs of your family perhaps? What did you do? How did things turn out?

Activity 3

Ask the class to think of a team name for the class. Make up or use known chants (several) using the class's new name. Make posters, mottoes, to form a group identity. These activities should produce a better, more cooperative atmosphere in class.

3 Doing

Evaluation

Activity 1 and 2

Assess students' answers and select some responses or texts to stimulate a class debate. Observe students' participation in this, and help them learn cooperation for the common good.

Activity 3

Observe students' participation in the activity and note the level of team spirit. Carefully assess the causes of any problems For serious ones seek advice on strategy from your psycho-educational department or from other teachers.

Specific Resolutions

Tell students to try to notice when individual interests conflict with the group's interest.

To remember the benefits of working for the whole.

To decide action accordingly.

Abilities:
* To understand that we are unique individuals who want acceptance by others;
* To understand that this can bring tension, especially during the transitional years of growing up;
* To be patient with self and others during the growing process.
Number of Chapters: 6 (6 to 11).

Chapter 6
Mirrors and Masks:
Issues of Identity

General Information

Topic

The identity crisis.

Content

▸ The differentiation process.
▸ Trying on different identities or masks.
▸ Negative identity.
▸ A positive self-image.

Objectives

Knowing
▸ To understand the characteristics of the identity crisis.
▸ To understand that the identity crisis is normal in adolescence.

Accepting
▸ To view the identity crisis positively as part of the maturing process.
▸ To reject the loss of self-worth which can accompany puberty and lead to negative attitudes and behaviour.

Doing
▸ To recognise what may happen in an identity crisis.
▸ To learn how such crises can be managed.

Areas of Human Development to be Emphasised

- ▸ Psycho-sexual development.
- ▸ Acceptance of self.
- ▸ Learning to handle oneself.

Class Plan

1   Knowing

Motivation

Ask if students can identify with Charlie's desire to be more grown-up. Can they identify with the tension between him and his dad? What do they think of Lucy's behaviour?

Story context:

Charlie is struggling to separate his identity from his dad's. By helping someone else who is adopting a rebellious identity, he is better able to deal positively with his own.

Introduction

The chapter addresses the process of becoming the mature self.

Presentation

Key Ideas

- ▸ Tensions are common as young people develop separately from their parents.
- ▸ This tension can be addressed in a positive rather than a negative way.

Topic Development

A   The differentiation process

Explain that at some point children begin to become their own persons—their future self. They naturally begin to separate from their parents in certain ways, no longer seeing their parents as perfect, nor wanting to be exactly like them. They may have a different outlook, and, like Charlie, feel certain tensions with their parents:

Charlie felt annoyed—he was being treated like a baby. Angrily, he turned away from his dad. In fact, Dad had started to get on Charlie's nerves lately. In some ways, he thought, I'm just like him, but sometimes I feel so different.

…Several nights later, Charlie's dad asked, "How's that girlfriend of yours?"

Hmph. Dad still has a way of winding me up, Charlie thought. "Dad! She is not my girlfriend!" he protested.

"OK, OK,," said Dad. "Sorry! But you talk about her so much, I thought we had a little crush on our hands."

"A little crush!" cried Charlie. "I'm not a little kid!"

"All I said was—" Dad continued, but thought the better of it when he saw Charlie struggling to control himself.

All you said, all you said, Charlie felt like shouting back at him.

Students have probably thought, felt, and argued similarly with their parents.

B   Trying on different identities or "masks"

During differentiation, adolescents may try on different identities or "masks" to find out which one fits best—as in the story. Obviously, this refers not to essential identity elements (e.g. sexual identity) which do not change, but to superficial elements, such as personal deportment, etc. In the story Charlie's mother says:

"You've been trying on some masks too."...

"Me? What do you mean?"

Mum smiled. "Wanting to shave, trying to show you're different from Dad—they're masks too, you know. You're trying out different personas and exercising your independence. But don't worry," added Mum. "It's just part of growing up. And you are really maturing now—you've been very responsible the way you've kept up your job with Mr Travis without letting it get in the way of your school work."

Charlie realises that Lucy, when experimenting at being more grown-up with the older boys, *looked different, though: distant, not the person he knew.* Charlie's mother notes of Lucy's behaviour, *"Sounds like she's trying on a mask…She's trying on a different self. There's nothing wrong with that for a teenager. It's just that the mask she's chosen is a negative one. It's dangerous."*

C   Negative identity

The above remark indicates that Lucy is assuming a negative identity. Sometimes adolescents differentiate themselves from their parents rebelliously through actions of which they know adults disapprove. This is not a truly differentiated self but a 'negative identity', formed by doing the opposite of what parents and society consider good. It's not the person's real self, but fake or inauthentic. This is why Charlie's mother urges him to *be her friend and show her that she doesn't have to put on a mask to be valued,* or to be herself. Charlie does so:

He wasn't quite sure how to do that, but he started by being nice to her and cheering her on in sports matches and gym events. Everyone probably thinks I'm madly in love with her, he thought. But he saw her simply as a friend.

D   A Positive Self-Image

Charlie helps Lucy develop a more positive self-image, so that eventually she stopped *hanging around with the guys outside the grocer's shop. Charlie wasn't sure if she had just tired of their company or realised that she valued her real friends more, but whichever it was, she looked happier.*

His own self-image is positive too. Looking in the mirror with his father, he feels at peace with their different images: *they looked at each other in the mirror and grinned. We look a lot alike, thought Charlie, but we are very different too. He was glad of both.*

Charlie is beginning to differentiate his own personality from his father's without having to turn against his father in order to do it or to assume a 'negative identity'.

2   Accepting

Guided Work

Ask the students to draw a self-portrait. What is their best feature? And their worst? Do they share any features with their mothers or fathers? Are they proud of any of the features they inherited from their parents? What about them is unique?

Activity 1

Ask the students to write 10 good things about themselves, and then to share their lists with a partner. Would the other person add anything? Would they add anything to the other person's list?

Activity 2

Ask each student to write one good thing about each of the other students on a card. Then distribute the cards to the students to whom they refer.

Activity 3

Ask students to imagine themselves making some negative remarks to friends, such as: *"You know, you'd be pretty good-looking if it weren't for that big nose."* Or to another friend: *"If it weren't for those extra pounds around the hips, you'd have a decent figure."* Or to another: *"You really messed up that basketball shot in gym today. Boy, did you look dumb!"* The point is that talking like this to friends rapidly drives them all away! Yet we often talk to ourselves like this.

Activity 4

Some psychologists estimate that people make negative statements about themselves several hundred times a day! Students can practice 'being their own best friend' by eliminating such negative self-talk.

3   Doing

Evaluation

Did the students treat the exercises seriously and do their answers show understanding? Ask them to name ways in which a teenager might adopt a negative identity.

Specific Resolutions

Ask students to try to be calm and assertive with parents (not aggressive) when tensions arise, as Charlie eventually became. No slamming of doors or running away, but a simple assertion, such as "I guess we're different in that way".

Recommend that they be appreciative of the gifts of personality their parents have given to them and that they tell their parents so.

Chapter 7
Friends and Family

General Information

Topic

The conflict of loyalties between friends and family.

Content

- The family as the school of love and relationships.
- The importance of peers.
- Balancing the two.

Objectives

Knowing
- Understanding that friendship and loyalty to friends is compatible with loyalty to family.
- Acquiring the skills to resolve apparent conflicts between the two.

Accepting
- Cultivating willingness to harmonise these two loyalties.

Doing
- Learning to harmonise any conflicts amicably and well.

Areas of Human Development to be Emphasised

- Family relationships.
- Peer relationships.
- Balancing primary and peer relationships.

Class Plan

1   Knowing

Motivation

Ask students to imagine a 'perfect day'. What activities and people does it include? Family members? Friends? Both?

Story context:

Charlie's parents are trying to build more 'family togetherness' because his mother's new job has affected them all. This interferes with some of Charlie's plans with his friends. Eventually they achieve happy compromises.

Introduction

Balancing peer and family relationships.

Presentation

Key Ideas

▸   Both family and peer relationships are important at this age.

▸   Family is the foundation for good relationships, including peer relationships.

Topic Development

A   The family is the school of love and relationships

The family has been called "the school of love", since it is where people learn how to relate to others, including those outside the family.

At this age students may feel much more drawn to peers than to family. Emphasise however that successful friendships (and all other relationships) have their roots in the family, where people learn loyalty, honesty, kindness, consideration, and all the virtues that make for good friendships.

Charlie can form and keep friendships because his is a warm and loving family:

Louis and Charlie asked if they could watch TV, and Mum said they could if they kept the volume down. Giselle got a book and read. Mum sat in her favourite chair and got out her sewing. It was really cosy. The oven gave off the most wonderful smell—it eventually woke Dad up.

"Do I smell something baking?" he asked, twitching his nose.

"Cakes!" shouted Giselle excitedly, waking Emily just in time for the first batch. The buns were delicious. Then Mum gave Dad a steaming cup of coffee and they were all enjoying themselves, chatting and eating, when the phone rang. Charlie picked it up. It was Ron.

Who would not enjoy being part of this family group? Charlie's friend, Ron, certainly does. He says: *"Your family is so special"*, and asks if he may join it.

A.1.   The Development of Empathy

Define empathy for the students, pointing out that it is quite similar to sympathy. It is the ability to experience the feelings, thoughts, and experiences of another person without having them directly oneself. If someone is in pain, an empathetic person almost feels the pain and can imagine and provide what the other person most needs for comfort. It is 'putting yourself in another person's shoes'.

Empathy is first learned in the play between mother and child. As the mother raises her eyebrows and says, "Goo, goo!" the baby will copy her gesture and try to make the same sound, even imitating the mother's emotions—excitement, joy, interest, etc. The quality of child/parent relationship—right from these early beginnings of empathy—is deeply formative of the capacity to relate well to others for the rest of life[1].

B   The importance of peers

Relationships outside the family are important too. Friendships contribute greatly not only to pleasure but also to personal development and success in life. Research by Willard Hartup shows that success in cultivating suitable, good quality friends (not merely having any friends) can be closely linked to success and happiness in later life[2].

Friendships provide emotional resources for having fun and dealing with stress. They help children's minds develop by providing additional knowledge and problem-solving skills. They teach a child how to enter a group, how to communicate and cooperate, and they train a child for future adult relationships in the home and on the job.

Children need friends for their hearts, minds, and social development. To be drawn to one another is natural. However, it is important to note that family relationships support many of the same things and can never be replaced by friendships alone.

C   Balancing the two

Typically for his age, Charlie and his friends make plans—which sometimes interfere with his family's needs. When Charlie wants to go to a film with a friend one Friday, his mother says, "I wanted you to babysit Emily tonight", but lets him go nevertheless.

On Saturday however *Mum said she and Dad wanted to go out together because they'd both been so busy lately they had hardly had any time for each other. She wanted all of the children to stay home and not have friends over. Charlie was annoyed because he had been planning to play football with his friends.*

Then Sunday, it is the same thing: *Charlie's parents said they all needed some 'family time' and that they were all going to go to the zoo. Charlie was loud in his protests.*

 But Mum didn't appear to be listening. "We need a day together, Charlie," she said. "Since I started this new job, our family has pulled apart a little bit, so we have to make a real effort to be together."

Charlie was in a bad mood. He slouched all around the zoo and even told Emily to get out from under his feet or he'd kick her. His Mum told him sharply to try to be pleasant.

Fortunately, Charlie is able to spend some time with his friends while at the zoo with his family: *"OK," Dad said. "There's a cafeteria ahead. Ask your friends if they want to join us." He glanced at Mum, who nodded. "Our treat," he added.*

Everyone seemed happy. Charlie was with his family, with his friends too. It was like one big family. When it was time to go, Charlie's feet hurt so badly from walking, he found he was glad to be going home with his parents.

---

1   Hojat, Mohammadreza. 'Satisfaction with Early Relationships with Parents and Psychosocial Attributes in Adulthood: Which Parent Contributes More?' *The Journal of Genetic Psychology, 159/2,* June 1998, pp 203-220.

See also Hojat, M; Zuckerman, M; Magee, M; Mangione, S; Nasca, T; Verage, M; Gonnella, J S. 'Empathy in medical students as related to specialty interest, personality, and perceptions of mother and father'. *Journal of Personality and Individual Differences, 39,* 2005, pp 1205-1215.

2   Hartup, Willard W. 'The Company they Keep: Friendships and their Developmental Significance'. *Child Development,* v67 n1, Feb 1996, p1-13.

See also Dunn, Judy. *Children's Friendships: The Beginnings of Intimacy.* Oxford: Wiley-Blackwell, 2004. ISBN 978-1405114486.

Charlie learns to talk in advance to his family about his plans, making them more open to compromise. Interestingly, when he is forced by circumstances to put family first, everything works out well: his friends can't come over at first, and he is enjoying an evening with his family. When friends come, it is an added bonus, not a necessity.

Point out the need to plan with one's family before planning things with friends. This will help parents be more compliant about plans with friends when they see that the priorities are right. Things will tend then to work out for the best.

Note that family relationships are called 'primary' relationships—that is, first in value or importance!

2   Accepting

Guided Work

Activity 1

Ask the students in groups of 3 or 4 to take turns being blindfolded. They must rely on the others in their group to guide them around the classroom from Point A (which is morning) to Point B (night). The teacher decides Points A and B.

Activity 2

Ask the students to make two lists: of the many ways of daily support they receive first from their family, secondly from friends. For each type of support, ask them to say whether they could manage without it.

Emphasise the need for them to return this support of family and friends, just as they helped the 'blind' person in their group.

3   Doing

Evaluation

Activity 1

After everyone has been blindfolded, mention that we never know what each day will bring. We rely on the help of others to accomplish all that we need to do during a day.

We could not spend a day without the support of others, especially our families. Check that they understand the importance of helping each other.

Activity 2

Ask some students to share with the class their lists from Activity 2 of Guided Work. Encourage them to find a balance between the two lists.

Specific Resolutions

To remember first to discuss plans with parents and family before finalising them with friends.

To value and contribute to 'family times'.

Chapter 8
Popularity and Personality

General Information

Topic

Popularity and self-esteem.

Content

▶ The natural desire for popularity, acceptance, and admiration.
▶ The effects of advertising.
▶ Inner beauty.

Objectives

Knowing

▶ Understanding the adolescent's need for popularity, and the feelings associated with it.
▶ Examining the adolescent's natural quest for self-discovery and self-confidence.

Accepting

▶ To give popularity its proper place, without overvaluing or undervaluing it.

Doing

▶ To avoid falling into a false sense of rejection or engaging in negative behaviours to avoid rejection.
▶ To avoid the pitfalls of 'selling' one's self and to value the person one is.

Areas of Human Development to be Emphasised

▶ Psycho-sexual and personality development.
▶ Self-knowledge.
▶ Self-acceptance.
▶ Self-management.

Class Plan

1 Knowing

Motivation

Ask students to close their eyes and ask them to raise their hands if they want to be popular. Then ask how many feel they are popular. When they open their eyes, explain that being popular is a very common concern among students of their age.

Story context:

With an Aesop fable as illustration, this story shows Alice falsifying herself so as to gain acceptance—she tastelessly tries on makeup and is tempted to shoplift to gain more prestige. Charlie encourages her to appreciate herself and her unique qualities. Mrs Alam, a teacher, encourages the students to resist commercial advertising and to resist 'advertising' themselves. Ask students to read the fable of the Jay and the Peacock:

> The Jay and the Peacock, by Aesop
>
> A jay, venturing into a yard where peacocks used to walk, found there a number of feathers which had fallen from the peacocks…He tied them all to his tail and strutted down towards the peacocks. Realising the trick, they pecked at him and plucked away his borrowed plumes. The jay could do no better than go back to the other jays, who had watched his behaviour from a distance. But they were equally annoyed with him, and told him, "It is not only fine feathers that make fine birds".

Introduction

The best 'you' is the real you—and that is the most attractive to others too.

Presentation

Key Ideas

▶ Aesop's fable of 'The Jay and the Peacock'.

▶ The false images 'sold' by advertising, and 'selling' oneself falsely.

▶ Being oneself rather than a false persona to impress others.

Topic Development

A   The natural desire for popularity, acceptance, and admiration

Point out that it is human nature to want to be liked. As social beings we care about each other and about others' opinion of us. We all seek and need other people's support and approval. This is normally a positive human characteristic.

Yet sometimes this natural desire makes us behave unnaturally just to fit in. Discuss the phoniness of the jay in 'The Jay and the Peacock': how it made his own friends turn against him; discuss the motto "It's not only fine feathers that make fine birds."

Point out that some people will go to any extreme to be liked and accepted by the crowd—even taking drugs or giving themselves away sexually if they think it will make them wanted. In a less extreme way, Alice is compromising. Charlie thinks:

Girls, thought Charlie—I'll never understand them. Here was Alice, going around looking like a lollipop, trying to look pretty and ending up looking like a clown. If her goal was to impress boys, she wasn't going to make it.

Charlie was taken aback to see Alice acting like that. It wasn't like her. Her friend Tiffany looked surprised too. Alice was laughing like a hyena with Mary and some of the more 'popular' girls.

Alice tells Charlie why she is acting like this:

"I'm scared of being left out."

Though she would do almost anything to be accepted, she does acknowledge that *"I don't want people to like me just because of my lipstick."*

Trying to be liked and noticed for the wrong reasons might include wearing the right 'look', even if it is unnatural, being overly sensual, acting a part, etc.

B   The Effects of Advertising

The media do not encourage us to be our true selves, and we are all influenced by sale tactics in magazines, newspapers, films, TV shows. Sometimes we get our ideas of human value from these powerful sources— which are often misleading. They appeal to something we naturally want—to be liked or admired— telling us that buying their products will fulfil this inner need.

Mrs Alam warns about advertising's deceptive side—how it manipulates people's natural desires so as to get their money:

She pointed out how advertisements manipulate people. She found an advertisement for a big, sleek, black car. Sitting on the bonnet was a beautiful blonde woman in a short, very tight black dress.

"Look what's happening here," said Mrs Alam. "The idea is to make men think that if they buy the car, they'll get the woman too. It plays on people's desire to be popular and loved. It seems to me the manufacturers should concentrate on making better cars instead of fancy advertisements."

Mrs Alam also speaks about advertising or 'selling' oneself:

"The same applies when you advertise yourself. You can spend all your time dressing up and showing yourself off to be popular, but that's something like selling yourself. You'd do better to concentrate on what kind of a person you are—your inner qualities will make you liked. You won't need to 'advertise', using sex appeal as the bait."

Perhaps Mrs Alam is speaking to Mary, a girl who is influencing Alice:

Mary was one of those girls whose figure had developed early. She wore her blouses so tight, Mrs Alam had given a lecture about it in class. "Mature, confident people don't need to advertise their bodies as if they were selling something," she said.

Alice says she understands. *"I do think Mary looks like she's selling herself cheap with those tight blouses. The looks the older boys give her—I'm not sure I'd want to be looked at like that. It seems kind of disrespectful."*

If we 'sell ourselves', or 'sell ourselves cheap', we are doing ourselves an injustice.

C   Inner Beauty

Mrs Alam assured the students that if they concentrate on being better people, their inner qualities will make them popular.

"True beauty comes from inside," she said. *"It comes from your character, your heart. Even the most beautiful people get old. If you only loved them for their looks, what would happen then? What lasts are things like honesty and trustworthiness. All the good looks in the world can't replace those. Now is the time, while you are young, to build up your inner strength. It will stand you in good stead throughout your life, in your future career, in your friendships, and later in married and family life. People who are beautiful on the inside are attractive to others."*

She says they should not neglect their outer appearance: *"Looking our best shows self-respect. It's nice for other people to be around a healthy, well-groomed person."* But she warns them not to overdo it, cheapen themselves or do anything false to achieve it.

Charlie reinforces the message when Alice tastefully updates her appearance.

"Just don't forget to emphasise your best feature," he said on the way home.

"What's that?" asked Alice, turning to face him.

"Your smile."

2   Accepting

Guided Work

Activity 1

Divide the class in groups of 4 or 5 students. Ask them to search through magazine advertisements and identify the human needs and desires they target. Ask each group to select one of the following attitudes:

The need for belonging

Acceptance

A desire for security

The need to feel *macho*

The need to feel seductive

Ask each group to identify, cut, and glue advertisements that target the attitude they selected; then, ask them to explain briefly their choice.

Activity 2

To give some perspective on popularity the teacher might discuss some famous media stars who seemed to 'have it all'—fame, fortune, talent, the adoration of crowds—yet ended up miserable because they lacked happiness in spite of their great popularity. For example:

Kurt Cobain—guitarist, vocalist, songwriter of multi-platinum rock group Nirvana. In the early 1990s, Cobain and his band became famous, instant millionaires. They were hugely popular, having the number 1 hit song of 1993. Kobain had a beautiful wife and child, riches, fans all over the world, and was an idol to many aspiring rock musicians. Yet by age 27 he had killed himself because of profound inner unhappiness.

Jennifer Capriati—tennis star. She won the Olympic gold medal in 1992, was admired, photographed, and had people following her adoringly all the time. Yet, in spite of her popularity, she was arrested for shoplifting in 1993 and for drug use in 1994.

There are many more famous stars who have had tragic personal lives in spite of great popularity with the public. Point out that some of these people never felt truly and deeply loved for themselves, even though millions of people 'loved' them for their looks and talent.

3   Doing

Evaluation

Each group should explain its collage.

After identifying the strong human needs that advertisers are targeting, students should list different ways people can satisfy those needs without buying the products.

Specific Resolutions

To recognise when the media are selling them something by appealing to deep inner needs which no product can possibly satisfy.

To find and use authentic means to fulfil the needs.

To detect lack of authenticity in oneself and others and to reject its influence.

Chapter 9
The Clique

General Information

Topic

Being true to self and one's ideals even when under adverse peer pressure.

Content

- Conformity/Peer Pressure.
- Integrity.
- Cliques.

Objectives

Knowing
- Accepting the importance of belonging to a group, but resisting peer pressure to control personal beliefs and actions.
- To show how group bullies often feel inferior themselves.
- To identify attitudes and activities of positive and negative groups.

Accepting
- To reject negative peer pressure.
- To value one's own convictions.

Doing
- Resisting the desire to conform at all costs.
- Rejecting peer pressure by avoiding conflicts, without compromising one's beliefs.

Areas of Human Development to be Emphasised

- Psycho-sexual and personality development.
- Manners and personal control.
- Assertiveness.

Class Plan

1 Knowing

Motivation

Ask the students their opinion of the story in the student book, in particular, what they think of cliques. What do they think of the pupils' code of not telling on one another?

Story context:

Alice is being pressured to join a clique that keeps others out by belittling them.

Introduction

Accepting some people in a group does not mean that others have to be excluded.

Presentation

Key Ideas

▸   Cliques are a painful adolescent reality.

▸   Shutting others out simply isolates the people in the cliques themselves.

▸   Conformity to peer pressure may be good or bad; it is important to discern.

Topic Development

A   Conformity/Peer Pressure—good and bad

Since humans are social beings with a tendency to conform, members of a society will gradually adopt similar habits of acceptable behaviour, dress codes, food preferences, speech patterns, styles of home, etc.

The strong influence we exert on one another is often good. However, human beings can be wrong too. If they conform to wrong things, a 'non-conformist' is needed to break the pattern and show a better way. Because the force of conformity is strong, however, conformists sometimes make non-conformists suffer.

Peer pressure can be good or bad. In Alice's story, it is bad because she is pressured to do something against her beliefs and which is harmful to others. If she conforms to this she will lose her *integrity*.

B   Integrity

Point out that integrity means adhering firmly to one's code of values; in essence it is the quality or state of being complete and undivided (from Latin *integer*—whole, morally upright).

It went against Alice's values to put some people 'down' for others to feel 'up'. She told Charlie that Mary and Rosa want her to join them in putting everyone else down, but *"I don't want to have to make other people 'out' so a few can be 'in.'"*

If Alice had acted against her conscience and violated her own values, she would have felt inner conflict, or been divided against herself, which is unpleasant. When we keep to what we believe to be true, we feel whole inside.

Integrity means being true to what one believes right, and constantly seeking the truth.

You could tell students about Sir Thomas More, who lived under King Henry VIII. He stands out in history as a man of great integrity. When asked to go against his deepest beliefs to satisfy his long-standing friend and monarch, King Henry VIII, he refused. The king wanted a divorce, which would create religious upheaval; Sir Thomas More disagreed. His property was confiscated, his family reduced to poverty, he was imprisoned, and finally executed, but right up to his death he quietly but steadfastly refused to compromise his beliefs. He did not rashly court death, believing the preservation of life to be an imperative as long as it could be done with integrity, but, when no path of escape remained without unfaithfulness to God and his conscience, he accepted the inevitable. (He explains this in detail, e.g. in his book *The Sadness of Christ*, which was written when he was imprisoned in the Tower of London).

Sir Thomas More was a great statesman, much admired in his own time. His execution caused outrage throughout Europe and he was later canonised (named a saint) by the Catholic Church. More recently, Pope John Paul II created him patron of statesmen and politicians *"because of the witness which he bore, even at the price of his life, to the primacy of truth over power"*.

Ask students, "Is being true to your beliefs and values always easy?" Of course, the answer is no.

When Alice first stands up to the ringleaders Charlie could see it was hard for her: *She was trembling slightly and her cheeks were bright red.*

It gets harder for Alice, too: *School became a nightmare for her...Finally Alice broke down and ran crying into the girls' cloakroom. Mary and Rosa followed, taunting her, and all the other girls went in too, just to see what was going to happen.*

Fortunately, with the support of her friend Tiffany, her cousin Charlie and a teacher, Alice does not give in. She defends and lives out what she believes to be good and true. Her rewards in the end, beside her own self-respect and a more integrated personality, are new friends and popularity.

Charlie tells her, *"You're the most popular girl in Year 8."*

In fact, Mary and Rosa change heart and ask Alice if they can join her circle of friends.

C   Assertiveness

Write this quote from Alexander Hamilton on the board: *"Those who stand for nothing fall for anything."*

It is important to act according to personal convictions. Yet there are ways to make one's position clear without rudeness. Being rude puts us in the wrong too. If Alice had been aggressive with Mary and Rosa, she might have said, "No, I don't want anything to do with you idiots!" If she had been too passive, she would have silently complied. Instead, Alice maintains her own politeness and manners but still does not give in:

"Alice!" Mary darted at her

Everyone stared at Alice.

"Yes?" answered Alice politely.

"Come and walk down the corridor with us."

It was a command, not a request. Alice searched for the strength not to obey. Just then, she caught Charlie's eye.

"I'm talking to Tiffany right now," said Alice.

Alice also maintains her politeness when Mary and Rosa come begging to join her service club. This keeps Alice in a position of dignity.

She looked round to see Mary and Rosa coming towards them.

"Alice, can we talk to you?" Mary asked.

Alice looked at them calmly and with dignity. "What do you want?" she asked evenly.

"Could we join your service club?"

Alice thought for a few minutes. Mary and Rosa were looking at her anxiously—as though they were afraid she was going to reject them. Alice guessed that they'd been lonely for the last few weeks, and that they genuinely wanted to join in.

"Yes, of course you can," she said. "I'm glad you asked."

It is important to assert our positions without rudeness but in a firm dignified way, so that we retain our self-respect and command the respect of others.

2   Accepting

Guided Work

Activity 1

Ask students to find quotes from the story to back up their answers to questions 1-4 of Activity 9 in their Student Book (p.221).

Activity 9

1.	Do students like Mary and Rosa in this story?
2.	Do they like Alice, Charlie, and Tiffany?
3.	What did they think of the girls who followed whatever Mary and Rosa said, even if they didn't agree with them?
4.	What did Charlie think of these other girls?

Activity 2

Ask the students to read the Inset about Mother Teresa in their Books (p.62). Ask students to name some famous non-conformists who changed things for the better.

> **Mother Teresa**
>
> You have probably heard of Mother Teresa. She features on every 'Most Admired Person' list. She was a Catholic nun, but people of many beliefs acknowledge her as a saint.
>
> To Mother Teresa, no one was 'out'. Everyone deserved to be respected and loved, even if they were living on the streets or in an alley. If a person was diseased or abandoned, Mother Teresa saw that as even more reason to love and care for them.
>
> When Mother Teresa received the Nobel Peace Prize in 1979, she accepted it in the name of "all those people who feel unwanted, unloved, uncared-for throughout society, people who...are shunned by everyone."
>
> Mother Teresa showed that by loving everyone a person may come to be loved by everyone.

Activity 3

Ask students to copy into their notebooks any quotations or examples from this chapter that they find inspirational.

Activity 4

Hold up an object such as a piece of chalk. Say, "This is a piece of cheese". Ask students to pass the chalk to one another, each saying while doing so, "This is a piece of cheese". Then ask: "Did calling this a piece of cheese make it one? Does what I say make a person acceptable or unacceptable, attractive or unattractive, cool or not cool?"

3 Doing

Evaluation

Ask students to give examples of good conformity and bad conformity to show comprehension. Ask them to write a short essay or speak about an incident when they showed integrity or stood up to peer pressure. Evaluate their comprehension from that.

Specific Resolutions

To memorise two good examples and apply them in real life peer pressure situations.

Daily self-questioning: "Was I true to my values and beliefs today? What improvements should I make?"

Chapter 10
What Makes the World Go Round?
—Magnanimity and Altruism

General Information

Topic

Magnanimity and altruism.

Content

▶ "No man Is an Island"—the social nature of human beings.
▶ Magnanimity and altruism bring happiness.
▶ Forgetting the self and concentrating on others.
▶ Dreams into reality.

Objectives

Knowing
▶ To understand magnanimity and altruism as ways to grow and be fulfilled.

Accepting
▶ To value magnanimity and altruism as basic human virtues which correspond to our need to reach out to others.
▶ To develop the desire to be outward looking and put others first.

Doing
▶ Learning to discern magnanimity and altruism in others.
▶ Looking for opportunities to be magnanimous and altruistic.

Areas of Human Development to be Emphasised

▶ Development of virtues.
▶ Relationship between happiness and helping others.
▶ Freedom and responsibility.
▶ Maturing in group dynamics.

Class Plan

1   Knowing

Motivation

Ask the students to interpret the story in the student book.

Story context:

Charlie discovers that helping a neighbour, his family, his cousin and schoolmates improves his world inside and out.

Introduction

Helping others makes the world better.

Presentation

Key Ideas

▶   Forgetting about self and giving to others helps both.

▶   In society and in nature the world works best through helping others.

Topic Development

A   **"No Man Is an Island"**

These famous words of poet and theological writer John Donne may puzzle the students. Try writing them on the board. Donne is writing figuratively to emphasise that no person is isolated, existing apart from humanity—all are interdependent.

Relate this to the point made in the last two lessons—chapters 8 and 9—that human beings are social by nature. We cannot separate ourselves from others. Isolation, loneliness, being cut off from others actually affect people's physical health. The healthiest, happiest people are those who have good relationships with others[3].

B   **Magnanimity and Altruism bring happiness**

Define these words as follows:

Magnanimity, from the Latin words for *great and spirit*, means the displaying of noble generosity.

Altruism is unselfish regard for, or devotion to, the welfare of others.

The happiest people are magnanimous and altruistic, since by giving we receive. It is like a broken circuit if we take without giving. Others need our generosity and help just as we need theirs. (Recall the 'Blindfold' exercise, where to get through each needed another's help.) The more we give the more we receive and the happier we are.

---

3.   Putnam, Robert D. *Bowling Alone: the Collapse and Revival of American Community*. New York: Simon & Schuster, 2000, Chapter 20, pp. 326-335.

     Waite, Linda J. and Gallagher, Maggie. *The Case for Marriage*. New York: Doubleday, 2000 (ISBN 0385500858), pp. 47-64.

C **Forgetting the self and concentrating on others**

However, if we give only in order to receive, that too breaks the circuit. We must give generously, without thought of self. Charlie gives to his family, Alice, and school in spite of a headache (he had read that the self was like a toothache and that it was best to forget about it and think about others). Others show gratitude and praise for his giving. This and his own helpfulness relieve his headache:

Charlie decided that he would try to forget his headache and be as nice as he could to everybody at breakfast. He took Mum and Dad their coffee and he got the milk for Louis and Giselle's cereal. Mum and Dad looked pleased, and everyone relaxed and started talking and laughing.

Charlie was surprised to find his headache was almost entirely gone. It was like that toothache, he thought— he had stopped thinking about himself and his headache, and it had almost cleared away.

Alice rubs his head after he helps her paint the cafeteria and the fumes re-aggravate his headache:

"You did something for me. So I'm doing something for you. We have to take care of each other."

Alice seemed to have a magic touch—Charlie found himself relaxing and feeling much better.

Then:

When Charlie got home, his Mum was in the kitchen preparing food. "Thanks for being so helpful this morning at breakfast," she said.

Charlie felt pleased. He'd had a really rewarding day despite his headache

At the beginning of the story Charlie doesn't particularly want to help the old lady. Yet he does so, forgetting about himself and his own wishes. He even refuses a monetary reward. But he still receives his reward for his selflessness:

Charlie was in high spirits for the rest of the afternoon. Time went by fast and he did not feel at all tired by the time he went home. Could that have been because he had helped the old lady, he wondered?

D **Dreams into reality**

Everyone has dreamed of a wonderful world without war, poverty, crime, or fear—a world of peace, plenty, happiness and joy. Whether it is more than a dream depends on each of us—how much magnanimity and altruism we show, how much joy and happiness we generate by our generous giving.

As an encouragement remind students that most volunteers and altruistic people almost always feel they get back much more than they give.

2   Accepting

Guided Work

Activity 1

Read and discuss "Nature's Way" in the student books (p.67):

Nature's Way–Symbiotic Relationships

Scientists once believed that parasitism (one species living off another to the other's detriment) was the main way of life in nature. Now they are finding now that symbiosis—living together cooperatively—is the way nature really operates.

For instance, there are cleaner fish in the ocean which clean other fish. Sometimes they remove their dead skin. Sharks allow fish into their mouths to clean their teeth (the fish must be brave!) The cleaner fish feed off the particles that they remove.

Birds called cattle egrets are attracted to herds of cows. The cows help the egrets by pawing up insects with their hooves for the egrets to eat. The egrets help the cows by landing on their backs and picking off any ticks and flies.

Helping one another is what makes the world go round.

Activity 2

Ask students to think of other examples of symbiosis (trees giving oxygen to human beings; human beings giving carbon dioxide to trees, for instance). Point out that the natural world mirrors the social world of human relationships.

Activity 3

Ask students to list the generous acts they have performed in the last week. Did they feel a natural high as Charlie did after helping the old lady?

3   Doing

Evaluation

Activity 1

Ensure that students understand the concept of symbiosis.

Activity 2

As a group activity, read the examples of symbiosis found by students.

Activity 3

Ask students to share with the class at least one of their listed good deeds and how they felt.

Specific Resolutions

Suggest to students that they try to give more to others without thinking of the return.

Ask them to notice when others are being magnanimous and altruistic and to note the positive effects of this.

Chapter 11
On My Honour

General Information

Topic

Truthfulness and acting honourably.

Content

▶ Honour: definition.

▶ Trustworthiness: a good reputation is better than gold.

▶ Building your future.

Objectives

Knowing

▶ Recognising the virtues which related to honour and genuineness.

Accepting

▶ To value being dependable, steadfast and truthful—these always bring personal fulfilment.

▶ To reject hypocrisy and insincerity.

Doing

▶ Recognising how practising sincerity and authenticity is shown in the attitudes and feelings of daily behaviour.

Areas of Human Development to be Emphasised

▶ Identifying with virtue.

▶ Relating virtue to happiness.

▶ Personal integration.

Class Plan

1 Knowing

Motivation

Ask students to recall silently whether they have ever been tempted to steal (most have)—and their thoughts at the time. They probably weighed up consequences. This story is about someone taking the consequences for a theft he didn't commit.

Story context:

Charlie, falsely accused of stealing, learns firsthand the value of an honourable reputation.

Introduction

Honesty pays in the end.

Presentation

Key Ideas

▸   There's no replacement for honesty.

▸   Dishonesty results in a tainted reputation and a less promising future.

▸   Honesty will win in the end.

Topic Development

A   Definition of honour

Define honour as: a good name, or public esteem; reputation for personal integrity.

The title of the story, 'On My Honour' means putting good name or reputation behind personal actions. This story deals with Charlie's good name jeopardised by a false accusation of stealing.

B   Trustworthiness: A good reputation is better than gold.

Charlie's grandfather used to say, "A good reputation is better than gold." Why?

Ask the students to imagine having a huge pile of gold, but having a reputation in their home village for having stolen it. Imagine bringing some of it into the village to make purchases: the looks and attitudes of the merchants toward the money and the supposed thief. Even if the 'thief' gives to charity, will they be grateful, or will they show contempt, believing this to be stolen money.

A good reputation will bring true friends, trust from neighbours, associates, employers, and other significant people. For instance banks will lend money to someone with a reputation for honouring debts. In many circumstances trust is better than gold.

C   A Good Track Record–Building the Future

Tell students that tomorrow—the future—is built upon their actions today. As Charlie's dad says,

"A track record, or your reputation, is really important in life. You've got to keep a clean track record, or people won't trust or respect you. You're building your future right now, and a big part of it is building a good reputation."

Charlie tries to build a better future—employment with local shopkeepers—when his reputation is ruined by the accusation of stealing:

Charlie decided that the best policy would be to lead a completely honest life, and hope that his integrity would eventually speak for itself. He would work hard to rebuild his good reputation so that people would trust him again.

Indeed, when the truth comes out about Charlie's honesty, not only does Mr Travis apologise and take him back at higher wages, but he has several other offers of employment from local shopkeepers:

Mr Travis was as good as his word, and Charlie began to get offers of work from

other shopkeepers. But he turned them down because he had already accepted

Mr Travis's offer of his old job—at a higher wage.

His grandfather was right, Charlie thought—a good reputation is worth more than gold!

2   Accepting

Guided Work

Activity 1

An excellent film on this topic is 'The Winslow Boy '—a true story. At a British boarding school a boy is expelled after an accusation of stealing. To restore the family's honour, the father asks the boy to tell him truthfully whether he stole the money in question. The boy truthfully answers no. From then on, all the family risk everything they have to defend their honour: money, time, even the daughter's engagement to a prominent man. The film may be a bit slow for twelve-year-olds, but excerpts could be effective.

Activity 2 'Two Facts and a Fable'

Students generally enjoy this activity! The students must each tell the group 'two facts and a fable' about themselves. The other students then guess which two are true and which is made up. An example might be a girl from Manchester who has four siblings, and loves football. She might say, "I am from Manchester, I have four siblings, and I hate football. Which is the tall story?"

Activity 3 "The Language of Virtues"

Ask students to look at Activity 11 in their Student Book (p.221), and match the words with their meanings by drawing a line to the correct match:

Activity 11

Honesty	regard for the standards of one's position, profession, or calling.
Honour	loyalty; stability; firmness.
Integrity	fairness; conformity to truth.
Steadfastness	incorruptibility; ability to be true to a trust, responsibility or pledge.
Justice	reliability; trustworthiness.
Dependability	a refusal to lie, steal, or deceive.

(Key:

Honesty = a refusal to lie, steal, or deceive

Honour = incorruptibility; ability to be true to a trust, responsibility or pledge

Integrity = regard for the standards of one's position, profession, or calling (this differs from the definition given in a previous chapter; point out that words often have more than one definition. 'Artistic integrity' would apply here.

Steadfastness = loyalty; stability; firmness

Justice = fairness; conformity to truth

Dependability = reliability; trustworthiness)

3 Doing

Evaluation

Activity 1

If you decide to watch the film, ask students to make brief comment, sharing it with the rest of the class.

Activity 2

After playing the game, students should consider which requires more mental gymnastics and a better memory: telling the truth or lying. They should realise that being honest is easier, makes sense, and is undoubtedly a good quality.

Activity 3

As a group activity, talk about each definition and its corresponding virtue.

Specific Resolutions

Ask students to adopt the motto "A good reputation is better than gold". They should strive to live up to it, realising that daily they are building their future.

Ask them also to reflect on the motto "Honesty is the best policy", and on its application in everyday situations.

Unit III:
My Family and My Future

Abilities:
* To understand that family remains the student's key support in the transitional years;
* To value each member of the family and manage the tensions which may arise at home;
* To understand and respect authority;
* To value the elderly.
Number of Chapters: 3 (12 to 14)

Chapter 12
Family Life and Strife

General Information

Topic

▸ Respecting and valuing the family.

▸ Maintaining autonomy and not allowing others to pressure one.

Content

▸ The meaning and function of the family.

▸ Love is what binds and motivates the family.

▸ Kindness goes a long way.

▸ Rewarding relationships.

Objectives

Knowing

▸ Understanding the meaning and mission of the family.

▸ Discovering that love is the beginning and main source of happiness in the family.

▸ Recognising the love underpinning relationships with parents and siblings—even when not immediately obvious.

Accepting

▸ Developing a positive attitude toward family, especially parents and siblings.

Doing

▸ Realising that kindness and helpfulness within the family make family life more caring and agreeable.

Areas of Human Development to be Emphasised

▸ Maturation in group dynamics: the family.

Class Plan

1   Knowing

Motivation
Story context:

Charlie's family is going through some everyday strife, especially his sisters, Giselle and Emily. At school he learns the value of the family, and at home sees how give and take bring peace and harmony.

Introduction
Family life can be hectic, but it fulfils our deepest needs.

Presentation
Key Ideas

▸ The family is irreplaceable as a source of strength, growth, and fulfilment.

▸ The family operates more smoothly when love is cultivated.

▸ Family relationships satisfy us at the deepest level.

Topic Development

A   The meaning and function of the family

In a quote from anthropologist Margaret Mead, Mrs Alam explains to sceptical Charlie that many people and societies have tried to change or replace the family but have failed: *"There is something about the family that really works wonders."* The family of two biological parents living together with their children is best for children's well-being. (This is now well-established. **For further information, see The Family Education Trust's website www.famyouth.org.uk which has useful links to other sites.**)

As some children in the class may not come from such families, emphasise Charlie's point about Ellie in Year 9. She is top of the class, happy and friendly, although her father deserted her and her mother. Emphasise that statistics and research show general trends—they do not apply to every family. Many children from broken homes do well, and many lone parents do their heroic best against difficult odds. Society as a whole should strive to support and help all kinds of families. But above all it should value, uphold and promote marriage and traditional families.

B   Love binds and motivates the family

Mrs Alam supposes that the secret of the family is love: *"Love helps people develop emotionally and mentally and in many different ways. Love is the first bond between people. You see that especially in the family."*

It is true that the love and support of family members makes life much smoother. Charlie has a humbling moment on the way home:

From what Mrs Alam had said, maybe he'd been judging his family too harshly. Maybe he got good marks and did well at his job and had friends and stayed out of trouble not because he was so great. Maybe it was because he had his family behind him.

C   Kindness goes a long way

Little acts of kindness bring great love and happiness to a family. Taught by their mother, Giselle has learned that giving a little special time to Emily makes her contented and less annoying.

Charlie also reminds Giselle that it is kinder to wash up her glass and bowl so their mother won't have to do it after coming in from work. They are confirmed in believing that it is worth being kind within the family when they note Emily's quiet contentment from Giselle's small kindness in buying a present and spending time with her.

D   Rewarding relationships

Giselle realises that Emily is not just a pest: *"She is a cute little thing, and she can be very sweet."*

Charlie also experiences intimacy with Giselle. He realises that his teacher was right about love, and the three siblings are happy and at peace with one another.

2   Accepting

Guided Work

Students may draw a genogram. This is a relational 'family tree'.

A square ☐ represents a male; a circle ◯ represents a female.

Their genogram starts with the parents:

☐ —————————— ◯

If the parents are living together, but not married, the line between them should be a broken one_ _ _ _ _ _ _. If they are separated, there should be a slash through the line _____/_____; and if they are divorced, two slashes through the line___//_____. If there is a remarriage, the partner is depicted on the other side of the wife or husband as a square or circle, but smaller than the original parents.

The children of the family come down from the parents' line and are drawn according to the square for male, circle for female pattern:

Stepchildren would be depicted with two lines down from the parents' line, one of them broken, and a foster child would be depicted by a broken line.

Next, the relationships are depicted. (In a different colour) students draw a line between each person and each other person in the family. If the relationship is fine, the line is simple and straight. If the relationship is very close, they draw two lines between the parties. If the relationship is distant, they draw a broken line. If the relationship is hostile, they draw a jagged line between the two parties.

They need not show these genograms to anyone. The purpose is to look at their family relationships, see which ones are good and which ones need to improve. Part of their resolution can be to improve those relationships within their control.

Activity 2

It has been estimated that a quarter of the work done by men worldwide is unpaid, and two thirds of that of women. Ask the students to think about what this work is and who does it—that of mothers and fathers in the home is obvious, especially that of mothers who stay at home looking after small children; but there are also magistrates, volunteers on many committees, such as in local government and for school governing bodies. Voluntary work is done for churches, for charities, in hospitals and prisons. The list is much more extensive than they may realise. Ask them to think what difference it makes whether work is paid or not (flexible hours, priorities when work and family life conflict, kudos given, quality of person in the job etc).

3 Doing

Evaluation

From this lesson students should gain a renewed appreciation of the family, and some determination to help their family succeed—both now and in the future.

Discuss which aspects of the genogram exercise were most useful to them.

Specific Resolutions

To appreciate the value of the family.

To try to be an asset to the family by performing small kindnesses to promote love and good feeling.

Chapter 13
Who's In Charge?

 ## General Information

Topic

Respecting and using authority.

Content

▶ Understanding authority: how it is conferred and held.
▶ Wielding authority well.
▶ Parental authority.

Objectives

Knowing
▶ Understanding that authority is really a position of service.
▶ Recognising the moral imperative of obedience.

Accepting
▶ To obey and wield legitimate authority.

Doing
▶ To recognize and respect legitimate authority in daily life.

Areas of Human Development to be Emphasised

▶ Group maturity.

Class Plan

1   Knowing

Motivation

Invite the students to retell the story in the student book.

Story context:

Charlie explores issues of authority—how it is conferred and held—by observing and questioning his parents and by self-observation.

Introduction

Wielding authority means accepting responsibility for others.

Presentation

Key Ideas

▶   The one who invests the most in an area is the natural authority.

▶   Authoritarianism is not real authority.

▶   Authority is best wielded with respect for those under one's authority.

Topic Development

A   Understanding authority: how it is conferred and held

Charlie's dad explains that in their family the mother is 'boss' in some areas and the father in others. Each case is decided by the amount of work and investment by each:

"If you are focused on something, you're obviously better able to make decisions. Of course, it's got to do with skills and interests, too."

It might be good to discuss the division of labour and authority in Charlie's home and in the students' homes. Who is in charge of what? Does working hardest in an area confer a natural authority on people in their families?

Explain that being the boss has its burdensome side. You might give as an example the true story of parents whose teenage son had already undergone extensive chemotherapy for a brain tumour. One consultant said that the remaining tumour should be left because removing it would be so difficult it could cause death or brain damage; another consultant recommended operating, saying that it might well grow again and be impossible to remove in future. The father asked his wife to let him as head of the family make the decision on the basis that he would bear responsibility if something went wrong. In the event, the wife refused to let him take sole responsibility but his lead will have helped her to a decision. The operation went ahead and, despite some lesser side-effects, was successful.

In case students think they may disobey authority not seen by them to be working hard, explain all the work done behind the scenes in school, for instance, or in a city or nation.

Charlie mistakenly thinks: *"It's us who work the hardest at school, so shouldn't decisions about that be ours?"*

His father points out that people *"who are working hardest to make our country succeed"* have decided that people need to be educated in order to be good citizens. The students cannot see all the work the principal, teachers, supervisors, city officials, etc, do. They often do not realise how hard their own parents work. Therefore, they should have an attitude of general respect toward adults and those in authority.

B Wielding authority well

Charlie learns the hard way that his siblings don't like to be ordered around harshly and that they don't recognise his authority when he does so. His mother advises him:

"You have to treat the people you're in charge of with respect and love. No one likes to be ordered about. It never hurts to speak politely to people—in fact, it's the only way."

However, people do need to be educated in respecting authority; it is not automatic, and some will take advantage of a soft-spoken, polite authority. Charlie's mother recognises that she needs to speak to Giselle and Louis and Emily to tell them how much responsibility Charlie has with his extra job, doing the most chores, etc. At the same time, she asks him to recognise how she and his father use authority:

"I think most of the time we ask you to do things rather than tell you to, and we try to show our concern and care in many different ways so that you know what we're asking you to do is for the best. .... Remember, authority is given to a person to help others grow and develop. When they realise you have their best interests at heart, you will earn their respect."

Charlie learns to speak politely but firmly to his siblings and gets a much better response. In fact, he is rewarded when his younger brother spontaneously and cheerfully tells a friend that Charlie is 'the boss!'

C Parental authority

Probably it is their parents who most love and care for the students. This gives parents a natural authority. In fact, good parental authority is a model for authority of all sorts.

Ask students to read the Historical Information provided in the student book (p.88):

Historical Information:

The greatest bosses and leaders are known to have had an attitude of caring and service towards those they led; so much so that people often thought of these great leaders as parents, not just leaders.

Mohandas K. Gandhi, the leader of India's independence movement, was called 'Bapu', which means 'Papa'. Abraham Lincoln, who led the people in the fight against slavery during the American Civil War, was called 'Father Abraham'. 'Mother' Teresa was called so by people from all over the world.

Alexander the Great, in the 4th century BC, is known as one of history's greatest leaders. His men followed him to unheard-of countries. He was the first to go into danger. He showed his care for his soldiers by never eating until they had all eaten, and tending to the wounds of each man. These actions earned him great loyalty from his soldiers, who demonstrated such bravery under his command that they were considered unbeatable.

Emphasise that people think of truly great leaders as 'parents' to their followers. This shows that 'parent' is the most fundamental honour and authority a person can have.

Alexander the Great is a good example of this type of 'parental' leadership. When leaders or parents display such good care and concern, those under them may be inspired to achieve greater heights.

2   Accepting

Guided Work

Activity 1

Students may role-play the scenarios in Activity 13 in the student book (p.222), demonstrating a 'wrong way' to ask someone to do something and then a 'right way'—the latter eliciting a compliant response.

Activity 13

> Think of some nicer ways to ask people to do the following things:
>
> "Do the dishes!"
>
> "Stop pestering the dog—now!"
>
> "Turn the TV off this instant!"
>
> "Get off the phone!"
>
> "Stop standing in the doorway!"

Activity 2

Ask students to discuss the qualities which make good parents natural authorities.

3   Doing

Evaluation

Activity 1

For the group project, ensure that students understand the difference between the right and wrong way to ask for things, and that they choose the correct way.

Activity 2

In class, ask students for examples of the parental qualities—so as to show how much of the chapter's content they understand.

Specific Resolutions

To recognise, obey and exert legitimate authority.

To realise that the authority's legitimacy may not always be readily understood.

To show respect for those in positions of authority.

Chapter 14
The 'Generation Gap'

 ## General Information

Topic

Respect for experience.

Content

- ▶ The value of elders.
- ▶ Don't judge by appearances.
- ▶ Our common humanity.

Objectives

Knowing
- ▶ Learning that experience is the best teacher.
- ▶ Understanding that old and experienced people can give excellent advice.

Accepting
- ▶ Realising the value of talking to trustworthy older, more experienced people.

Doing
- ▶ Initiating conversations with known adults.

Areas of Human Development to be Emphasised

- ▶ Group maturity.

Class Plan

1 Knowing

Motivation

Story context:

Charlie dislikes old people, but a visiting Grandpa's love and wisdom win him over.

Introduction

The elderly may seem boring, but from long experience they teach and give much.

Presentation

Key Ideas

▶ The elderly are wise in life and love.

▶ Their advice can make young people's lives better.

▶ They should be respected and valued as rich sources of history and experience.

Topic Development

A The value of elders

In the story Charlie, Louis, and Giselle don't know why they should respect their elders, only that they've been told too many times.

"What's so important about this guy?" Charlie asked Giselle.

"Well, he is very old, and if no-one's there to meet him, he might get lost."

"Oh, this is going to be real fun," groaned Charlie.

Louis rolled his eyes, as if to agree with Charlie, but Giselle caught herself. "It's only for two weeks," she said. "We need to respect the older generation."

"Why?" asked Louis.

"I don't know," said Giselle.

"Well, they're supposed to be wiser," Charlie said. "But, if that's true, why have they left us this crummy world to grow up in—full of poverty and crime and war and pollution?"

Charlie, in particular, has difficulty in respecting elders; in fact, he's downright hostile:

Charlie did not really like old people. Sometimes they smell, he thought, and they always want to hug and kiss you. They shout because they can't hear how loudly they are talking. And they cup their hands behind their ears and say, "What? What?" to everything you say. One or two drove him nuts at the shop—they were always in the way in the aisle, and they never seemed to know when there was someone behind them trying to get through. A lot of them have outlived their usefulness, he thought, and with getting sick all the time and having to be helped, you wonder if they wouldn't be better off just keeling over.

Both Charlie and the reader discover that 'Grandpa' knows much about life and love.

"You're troubled," Grandpa said.

Wow, those bright old eyes missed nothing. "No," Charlie replied. "Just tired."

"Oh," he said. "Nothing more?"

He seemed to know just what Charlie was thinking!. His eyes were twinkling, and his toothless mouth was twisted into a knowing smile. Charlie felt he could trust him—and suddenly wanted to tell him everything.

Charlie wants to know more about life from his Grandpa:

Charlie asked him if he would mind if he wrote to him and asked his advice on things sometimes. He said he'd be very pleased.

When Grandpa is gone, Charlie misses him sorely.

Grandpa had a special ability to make Charlie feel important. The others had felt it too. Where did he get that ability from?

"From a good long life," said Dad.

Charlie extends his feeling for his 'Grandpa' to old people in general:

From then on, Charlie found his attitude towards the old people in the shop and on the streets changed. He no longer saw them as has-beens who had nothing to offer. He saw them as a source of wisdom and experience, from whom he had a lot to learn.

Good family relationships help children project their love for family members onto society in general. They relate warmly, trustingly, and respectfully to older men and women, who remind them of their mothers and fathers. Aunts, uncles, grandparents, and great-grandparents all help children relate to others of similar age and position.

Encouraging students to respect and appreciate family members imbues them with the social facilities they will need to operate successfully and happily in society.

B   A Crabby Old Woman

Consider the following poem. Perhaps it could be read aloud in class or copied for students to read. It is written by an elderly woman, explaining her life and begging those who deal with her in her old age to respect her as a person like themselves.

A Crabby Old Woman

What do you see, nurses, what do you see?
Are you thinking when you're looking at me:
A crabby old woman, not very wise,
Uncertain of habit,with far-away eyes,
Who dribbles her food and makes no reply
When you say in a loud voice, "I do wish you'd try!"
Who seems not to notice the things that you do
And forever is losing a stocking or shoe—
Who unresisting or not lets you do as you will
With bathing and feeding, the long day to fill?
Is that what you're thinking? Is that what you see?
Then open your eyes, nurse, you're not looking at me.
I'll tell you who I am, as I sit here so still,
As I move at your bidding, as I eat at your will.
I'm a small child of ten with a father and mother,
Brothers and sisters who love one another;

A young girl of sixteen with wings on her feet,
Dreaming that soon now, a young man she'll meet.
A bride soon at twenty: my heart gives a leap,
Remembering the vows that I promised to keep.
At twenty-five now I have young of my own
Who need me to build a secure happy home;
A woman of thirty—my young now grow fast,
Bound to each other with ties that should last.
At forty my young sons now grown will be gone,
But my man stays beside me to see I don't mourn.
At fifty once more babies play round my knee
Again we know children, my loved one and me.
Dark days are upon me, my husband is dead.
I look at the future; I shudder with dread.
For my young are all busy rearing young of their own,
And I think of the years and the love I have known.
I'm an old woman now and nature is cruel:
'Tis her jest to make old age look like a fool.
The body it crumbles, grace and vigour depart.
There is now a stone where once I had a heart.
But inside this old carcass a young girl still dwells,
And now and again my battered heart swells.
I remember the joys, I remember the pain,
And I'm loving and living life over again.
I think of the years, all too few, gone too fast,
And accept the stark fact that nothing can last.
So open your eyes nurses, open and see,
Not a crabby old woman. Look closer—see me.

This poem was written by 'Kate'—an old woman in hospital in England who could no longer speak. When she died, this poem was among her belongings. It later appeared in the Christmas edition of *Beacon House News*, a magazine of the Northern Ireland Mental Health Association.

C Our common humanity

Because life is new to them, sometimes young people feel that no-one has ever before had their experiences or feelings, and that no-one understands—things were too different when their parents and grandparents were young. Emphasise that this is a fallacy. People have loved, become rich, lost everything, experienced troubles and joys, had hopes and dreams for as long as people have been on earth.

The old saying 'Let's not re-invent the wheel' could be put on the board and discussed. To ignore the wisdom and experience of elderly people is continually to re-invent the wheel. Those who have already experienced life and love can teach us much.

2 Accepting

Guided Work

Activity 1

Ask students to answer the questions from Activity 14 in their Student Books (p.228).

Activity 14

1. Have you ever prejudged an old person based on their physical weaknesses? Did you discover that there was more to the person than met the eye?

2. Has an old person ever played an important role in your life—giving you love and/ or advice?

3. How does Charlie's attitude toward old people change over the course of the story?

Activity 2

Empathy for those who have gone before can be encouraged through old photographs—perhaps of wedding couples, old film stars when young, historic photos, etc. This humanises people whose heyday is past. Point out their facial expressions, their likely emotions. What were this young bride's hopes when she married? Or this soldier's feelings at going to war? Excerpts of old diaries can also 'humanise' people of the past and help young people see that these people had similar feelings to theirs.

3 Doing

Evaluation

Activity 1

Hold a class discussion about their answers to questions in Activity 14. Encourage students to develop empathy for adults.

Activity 2

Assess students' reactions to the old photographs and stories.

Specific Resolutions

To respect and honour older people.

To learn from their wisdom and experience.

Abilities:
* To understand what it means to be a true friend;
* To develop a habit of loyalty to friends and family as a foundation for future relationships, including marriage;
* To understand boy/girl relationships, and why discipline pays off;
* To begin thinking about jobs and careers.
Number of Chapters: 8 (15 to 22)

Chapter 15
Romeo and Juliet?

General Information

Topic

The qualities of friendship as the basis for love and marriage.

Content

▸ The basis of love.
▸ The basis of friendship.
▸ The interrelationship between the two.

Objectives

Knowing
▸ Realising that friendship, as the basis of love, needs cultivating.
▸ Recognising friendship as the basis for any future love.
▸ Realising that false imitations of love lack the vital ingredient of friendship.

Accepting
▸ Throughout life to treasure friendship.
▸ To reject phony relationships that 'use' or 'buy' people.

Doing
▸ To use opportunities for making friends and deepening friendships.

Areas of Human Development to be Emphasised

- Group maturity: friendship.
- Group maturity: the couple.

Class Plan

1   Knowing

Motivation

Ask students whether they want many friends, or to learn the key to friendship.

Story context:

Charlie explores love and friendship through conversations with his parents, a class on Romeo and Juliet, and in relationships with classmates.

Introduction

True love has its foundations in friendship.

Presentation

Key Ideas

- What passes for 'love' may be illusory.
- Love is based on friendship qualities.

Topic Development

A   The basis of love

You could summarise the plot of *Romeo and Juliet*—one of the most famous love stories ever. The play concerns the basis for love. Is this merely physical attraction?

In this chapter the students, in discussing the basis of Romeo and Juliet's love, mention friendship, loyalty, commitment and not using a person. They could also have mentioned the marriage relationship as a means of peace and reconciliation within and between families, and in society (the play fosters this hope). At the deepest level true and lasting love is based on a sense of the sacred, of venerating the other person—particularly the woman by the man. Romeo calls Juliet "this holy shrine" and "dear saint": the beauty of her virtue is what he immediately perceives and admires, what makes her different from all other women he has met. This attitude is not a substitute for religious devotion, but properly sees created (human) life as sacred, to be treated with great reverence and honour. Love in Shakespeare is often treated in this way (Ferdinand and Miranda in *The Tempest* are another example), and it follows a long, widely held tradition and belief—attitudes based on concepts of chivalry and courtesy, which had a strong religious dimension: in the Christian tradition this in particular took the Blessed Virgin Mary as a pattern and example, but other faiths have similar patterns[4].

---

4.   For a deeper discussion of this, the following article is worth reading: Bruten, Avril. 'The Courtesy of Our Lady: a Mediaeval View'. *Second Spring*, Issue 1, 2001 (available on-line).

There is also the concept of complete gift of self and all one has—of total, devoted service—which is integral to true and lasting love. The woman in particular may see herself in this dimension, but it applies to both. Students may question how Romeo and Juliet may be so sure of one another's character and of their love just by looking at one another. Renaissance neo-Platonic theory—followed by Shakespeare—held that outward appearance, particularly eyes, was a sure guide to inner character. There is much to commend this, if exercised with due care and penetration.

Often, our own age values man/woman relationships only for what each can get out of the relationship, and this is partly why so many do not last—so it is very beneficial to study the attitudes in Shakespeare and other great writers of the past: to recapture a sense of the sacredness and beauty, moral and physical, of young love.

Sara is physically attractive—so much that Charlie wants to be seen with her as if she were a 'trophy'. His father warns him not to 'use' her as a flattering mirror of himself. Point out that if we want people in this way, it is really only self-love. Much so-called 'love' is self-centred. Emphasise that true love is based on caring about the other person. It is based on wanting to support, promote and benefit that person, not oneself. Therefore, we must respect the other, with high regard for the real inner person.

In love, pleasing looks alone are not enough: the person within is what really matters. Charlie acknowledges that really he and Sara have little in common. Charlie's dad also mentions, *"I'm not going to deny that I thought [your] Mum was pretty. But I've met some very pretty women I wouldn't want to spend much time with, let alone a lifetime."*

B   The basis of friendship

We 'love' our friends for the real person beneath the surface, rarely just for outer appearance. The inner qualities of character we seek in our friends include, above all, loyalty. As the students say, a good friend is:

"Someone who will stick with you through thick and thin."

"When you need them they're there."

"They stand up for you."

"They don't talk about you behind your back."

C   The interrelationship between the two

Point out that love and friendship are both built on qualities of good character, including loyalty—which is similar to commitment; it means being there for one another, not betraying one another, supporting the other person, even if absent. (Note that Juliet calls Romeo "husband, friend").

Friendship: no physical attraction, may be same sex, non-romantic (platonic feelings).

Love: physical attraction, opposite sex, romantic feelings.

Both: loyalty, trustworthiness, honesty, kindness.

2   Accepting

Guided Work

Activity 1

Ask students to take the Loyalty Test in Activity 15 in their student books (p.223).

Activity 15

Are you a loyal friend? Take this test and see.

(Answer Yes/No)

1. I stand up for my friend even if it means bucking the crowd and risking my own 'cool' image.

2. I never tell my friend's secrets to others (unless my friend or someone else is in danger or trouble because of those secrets).

3. If I say I am going to do something with or for my friend, I try very hard to do it, even if it's not what I want to do at that moment.

4. I'm honestly happy when something good happens to my friend.

5. I'm honestly sad if something bad happens to my friend.

6. I try to forgive my friends their shortcomings

7. My friends and I can disagree about something and still respect each other's opinions.

8. I stand up for my friends if they're criticised, or when they are not there to defend themselves.

9. If my friend needs me, I put my own interests aside to help him or her.

10. I've had the same friend or friends for years.

Scoring: The more 'yes' answers you had, the more loyal a friend you are. You probably have at least one very close friend and maybe several. Your friends will very likely remember you, even if you move away from each other. For any 'no' answers, you need to work on these areas. It takes practice to be a good friend or spouse.

Now ask a friend to answer yes or no about you to these questions. Did your friend rate you as you rated yourself? Maybe you are more (or less!) loyal than you think. Keep working at it!

Activity 2

Share ideas on how to get to know someone as a friend. What kind of questions do you ask? How do you assess whether someone is a good potential friend or not?

3   Doing

Evaluation

Emphasise that loyalty and good character are vital both for friendship and true love. Marriage is a great, lifelong friendship. Building good friendships and having the necessary character qualities will help students later to build strong, happy marriages.

Activity 1

Review the results of the Loyalty Test with the class.

Activity 2

Analyse with students the characteristics they mentioned when pooling ideas. Lead them to realise the importance of asking the right questions to find true friendship.

Specific Resolutions

Not to be deceived by looks alone, but to learn to look for inner qualities.

To build the inner qualities of a good friend, knowing that these are the basis for becoming a good spouse in the future.

Chapter 16
Charts and Chilli Peppers

General Information

Topic

Dating; choosing a spouse.

Content

▶ Dating is not just for having a good time.

▶ Courtship is preparation for marriage.

▶ What to look for in a dating partner.

▶ Physical restraint during dating.

Objectives

Knowing

▶ Distinguishing dating from friendship.

▶ Dating is a preparation that will lead to engagement and later marriage, so it needs to be handled with great respect.

Accepting

▶ Dating should encourage love for one another; this should always be done with respect and clear purpose.

Doing

▶ Friendships with those of the opposite sex should be kept within proper bounds.

▶ Knowing how to keep 'dates' at a level of respect, which helps the two to know each other better.

Areas of Human Development to be Emphasised

▶ Group maturity: the couple.

Class Plan

1   Knowing

Motivation

Ask students if they approve of the use of drugs. Ask them if they have ever thought of 'being in love' as being on drugs.

Story context:

The literature class continues to discuss issues raised by Romeo and Juliet—love, dating, marriage, and physical attraction.

Introduction

The purpose of dating and the bounds of physical affection in a dating relationship.

Presentation

Key Ideas

▸   Dating is serious business, to be undertaken with marriage in view.

▸   Physical involvement clouds the issues.

▸   Before dating it is important to get to know the other person's character.

Topic Development

A   Dating is not just for having a good time

People naturally want to enjoy going out together, but how is this achieved? If they feel worried, guilty, sick, used, violated or in danger of some sort afterwards, this is not a 'good time'. Good times happen for people who respect one another, support one another's best interests, and are free to laugh and have fun since they can be accepted for the people they are. Dating should involve feelings of this kind, as well as the stimulation of being in the company of the opposite sex.

The story advises that the more hours young people spend alone with someone of the opposite sex, the earlier on they are likely to have a sexual encounter. To protect themselves from unpleasant consequences, intense one-on-one dating should be put off as long as possible. It is usually much more fun to be in a group.

B   Courtship—preparation for marrying

As feelings between those of opposite sex can be intense, dating should be treated as courtship—preparation for marriage; significant adults (parents) should be involved. The vast majority understand their children's real interests—unlike Romeo's and Juliet's families. Life usually does not have all the elements of Shakespearean tragedy!

Dating without seriousness is like playing with fire. Fire is very powerful, making life much better as long as it is properly contained. A candle, a fire in the fireplace, a campfire are wonderful. But a house on fire, or a forest fire, is a fire out of control and very dangerous. Sexual attractions are like fire—good and life-enhancing if kept within safe limits and control. Seeing dating as courtship—preparation for marriage with parental help and approval in selection—contains attraction within safe boundaries.

C   **What to look for in a marriage partner**

Mrs Alam advises about 'dating': *"Watch how he or she treats others, because the key isn't how the person treats you—it's how he or she treats others. Is he or she polite and helpful? Kind? Generous? Patient? All these qualities count for so much in marriage. That's why I told you yesterday that you should be building up your own virtues and characters now in order to have good marriages later. In the same way, you should keep in mind that a virtuous person is the best candidate to be looking for."*

Being fun, attractive and stimulating is little use if underneath someone is cruel, careless of other people's feelings, goes out with many different people but pretends to be seeing only one—that makes for a very painful situation. Students should learn to look for someone who is attractive not only outwardly but inwardly too. General attitudes should be considered, as should attitudes to money, treatment of animals and relationships with both sets of parents.

D   **Physical restraints during dating**

1. Boy and girl meet Attraction	2. Talk, discuss and get to know each other well	3. Decide they are well-suited to each other	4. Make a commitment (marriage)	5. Get physical. Produce endorphins and oxytocins that bond them and blind them
1. Boy and girl meet Attraction	5. Get physical. Produce endorphins and oxytocins that bond them and blind them	3. Decide they are perfect for each other	2. Talk, discuss and get to know each other well	4. Discover that they are not very compatible after all—leading to an unhappy commitment or unhappy break up.

Mrs Alam explains that the body releases natural chemicals, or endorphins, when it is affected by certain pleasures—massaging the scalp, cartoons, even eating chilli peppers! But definitely it is stimulated by kissing and caressing. She explains: *"Physical involvement too soon doesn't help you to know the person: it clouds the issues. When you hold hands, when you kiss, a whole complex chemistry starts up in your body that can be overwhelming. You might feel madly in love with someone who just kisses well and is good-looking. But, in fact, you're not really in love at all."*

Spend time on the various stages of the chart. Emphasise how physical caressing releases chemicals that bond people and make them feel inseparable, even if they are completely wrong for one another. Explain that getting to know one another and making a serious commitment should precede caressing, which can lead to 'chemical bonding' between the two, deluding them into thinking they have an enduring love.

Psychologist Steven Stosny says of attachment: "Popular wisdom has always held that love is like an addiction and that losing attachment figures is like drug withdrawal syndrome. Now there is empirical evidence. The endogenous opiate system seems, indeed, to provide a pleasure reward for attachment and a withdrawal penalty for loss of the attachment bond."[5] (This would help explain Romeo and Juliet's tragic deaths).

2   Accepting

Guided Work

Activity 1

Ask students to recall the most important elements of the happiest times in their lives. Probably these were innocent times centred round people they truly liked and trusted.

Activity 2 (Optional)

In class show some clips from West Side Story and the BBC Shakespeare Collection *Romeo & Juliet* (1978): a beautiful, artistically faithful production. Explain to students that West Side Story is inspired by *Romeo and Juliet*, and set in New York.

The teacher might mention that the lovers' passion for one another is ignited by seeing each other at a dance. In class discuss cultural differences in the modern (Western) era that make it less likely that a relationship in such circumstances would endure now.

3   Doing

Evaluation

Again urge students not to be fooled into thinking they are 'in love' by 'feel-good' hormones released by the brain in physical caressing. Stress the withdrawal pain from these natural drugs when a relationship breaks up, as most youthful relationships do.

Activity 1

Ask students to share their thoughts on good times. Emphasise that a truly happy time is usually serene, and though it may be intense, it never leaves a bad impression.

Activity 2

Discuss how the characters save for marriage the sexual expression of their love. Try to show students how controlling their own passions is possible and beneficial. Point out that controlling passions means not only violent passions but also sexual passions.

Specific Resolutions

To treat dating with respect and care as preparation for marriage, involving parents in decision-making and guidance-giving.

To avoid physical affection until ready for commitment, and then to use restraint until marriage.

---

5.   Stosny, Steven. *Treating Attachment Abuse: a Compassionate Approach.* New York: Springer, 1995 (ISBN 0826189601), p.17.

Chapter 17
To Live Happily Ever After

 ## General Information

Topic

Marriage.

Content

▸ Marriage enhances true personhood and freedom.

▸ The importance of common goals.

▸ Ceremony and commitment.

Objectives

Knowing
▸ Understand what is needed for a dating relationship to move on to marriage.

▸ In hypothetical situations discerning irrational ideas about marriage and choice of spouse.

▸ Understand the symbolism concerned with marriage.

▸ Realising that a good marriage is not automatic but needs preparation.

Accepting
▸ A good marriage should be valued: it leads to personal fulfilment and happiness.

Doing
▸ Developing positive attitudes that will lead to a good marriage.

Areas of Human Development to be Emphasised

▸ Group maturity: the couple.

Class Plan

1   Knowing

Motivation

Ask students if any of them would like to be married some day.

Story context:

The literature class continues to discuss issues of love and, specifically, marriage.

Introduction

The commitment of marriage is a way to personal fulfilment and happiness.

Presentation

Key Ideas

▶   Marriage leads toward, not away from, freedom and fulfilment.

▶   Marriage is natural to humans: the oldest, most widespread social institution.

▶   Marriage is founded on commitment.

Topic Development

A   Marriage enhances personal fulfilment and freedom.

Write on the board these words of psychologist Ben Pittman for students to read and think over: *"Marriage is not supposed to make you happy. It's supposed to make you married, and once you are safely and totally married, then you have a structure of security and support from which you are free to make yourself happy."*[6]

In the story, Alan and some other boys think that marriage seems like 'a prison', while they want to be 'free'. Not only boys feel this: more divorces are initiated by women.

However, many people find, as Ben Pittman jokingly said, that marriage leads to happiness because of the support, sympathy, task- and resource-sharing that are part of it. For example, if one partner is sick or unemployed, the other can take on more work for a while. A marriage partner will listen, and give a sympathetic perspective on other people and situations. A partner in life, someone of the opposite sex whose strengths are different and complementary is an extremely valuable asset.

Many married people feel freer in relationships, especially with the opposite sex. Committed, settled in romantic and sexual questions, they no longer need be part of the jealousies, intrigues, agonies and uncertainties of single and dating people. Tell children that some adults call dating a 'meat market' as they feel bought and sold only for their bodies. Free from this pressure, married people, supported by their spouse, can interact pleasantly and purely with the opposite sex in social and work situations. Statistically, married people are happier, healthier, and wealthier than single people or the divorced.[7] This leads to greater personal fulfilment and freedom.

---

6.   Pittman, Ben. *Grow Up!: How Taking Responsibility Can Make You a Happy Adult.* New York: Golden Books, 1998. (ISBN 0307440648), p. 160.

7.   Waite, Linda J. and Gallagher, Maggie. *The Case for Marriage.* New York: Doubleday, 2000. (ISBN 0385500858).

B   The importance of common goals

Mrs Alam quotes author Antoine de Saint-Exupéry, *"Love does not consist in gazing at each other, but in looking outward together in the same direction."*[8] She advises students to seek a spouse whose values and goals match theirs in order to avoid the pain of divorce. Therefore it is vital they understand and now work on their own values and goals, helped and supported by their parents, mentors, heroes, and religious or spiritual leaders (Romeo and Juliet sought spiritual guidance from Friar Lawrence). Emphasise the importance of this.

A young couple may feel passionately in love (due to endorphins: see Chapter 16), and so may tend to gloss over differences, believing that 'love will find a way'. While all couples differ on some issues, simply learning to live with these unresolved, major differences in values and goals will be a big obstacle. Most couples when taking marriage vows believed that love would resolve differences, but the divorce rate— 60% of new marriages in some developed countries—tells a different story.

Emphasise that—according to psychologists and marriage experts—being intensely in love will inevitably lessen within a few years of marriage, and they should be prepared for it. At this stage it is essential to strive together for shared goals and values: then mutual respect will grow, and a more lasting and tender form of love ensue.

C   Ceremony

Point out that all societies known in history have had some form of marriage tradition and ceremony to announce and regulate sexual and domestic arrangements and care of children. Human nature tends toward sealing their unions with vows and ceremony. This is why social scientists are so concerned about the escalating trend of co-habitation. Co-habiting couples break up more easily, there is more violence between them, and more chance of sexual and other abuse of children who are not the biological children of both co-habitors in a household.

Discuss with students whether or not they think marriage is 'just a piece of paper', as Richard does in the story.

D   Commitment

Point out that marriage is a challenging undertaking. Like a house built with great effort. Marriages do not just happen, the ceremony does not automatically convey happiness. Though special, the ceremony is just the beginning of a lifelong endeavour.

Ask students if they have seen a boy and a girl's name carved into a tree or written into cement. Often the inscription will include a heart and the word 'forever'. True love has always been thought to last forever, as has sometimes friendship.

To grow, true love needs commitment. One author put this jokingly: *"One advantage of marriage, it seems to me, is that when you fall out of love with him, or he falls out of love with you, it keeps you together until you maybe fall in again."*[9]

Because love is not just a feeling (feelings are as changeable as the weather), commitment sees a couple through. They don't break up even if one of them is bad-tempered, or one has bad breath, etc. Staying together through thick and thin brings lifelong growth of true love. Perseverance is a large part of victory in love and in life.

Ask students to read the story of King Robert the Bruce (p.115 in their Books):

---

8.   Saint-Exupéry, Antoine de. In *Wind, Sand and Stars* (original title: *Terre des homes*), Chapter 9: Barcelona and Madrid, 1939.

9.   Pittman, Ben. *Grow Up!: How Taking Responsibility Can Make You a Happy Adult.* New York: Golden Books, 1998. (ISBN 0307440648), p.160.

Robert the Bruce (King Robert I of Scotland)

Robert the Bruce was crowned King of Scotland in 1306, and, from then on, he tried to rid Scotland of the English.

This was no easy task. After being badly defeated in a battle, Bruce hid in a cave for three months. He felt he had come to the end. He thought of running off to France or some other country and abandoning Scotland forever. He was ready to give up.

Then a spider caught his attention as it spun its web. The thread broke and the spider fell down time after time, but it kept creeping up and having another go, and at last it succeeded. The spider's perseverance inspired Bruce. He thought that if a spider could be that strong and determined, surely a man like him could be too. He adopted as his motto, 'If at first you don't succeed, try, try again'. He inspired his men with the motto and went on to fight for eight more years, eventually freeing Scotland from England.

2   Accepting

Guided Work

Activity 1

Ask students to make a 'Spouse Wanted' advertisement. They should imagine advertising for a spouse for a best friend or close relative, listing the qualifications needed by the potential spouse, thinking what kind of a person would be suitable to stay with forever. At the end, students review their lists and ask themselves whether they themselves measure up to their idea of a good spouse.

Activity 2

Ask students to describe briefly a time they were glad to have persevered at something—a sport, homework, playing an instrument, a friendship—even if it brought them many difficulties. What were the eventual rewards?

Activity 3

Ask students in small groups to recount to one another a ceremony they have taken part in. What was its purpose, and their role in it, the emotions it evoked, its meaning for them, its lasting memories? Ask them to select the best one to read to the class.

3   Doing

Evaluation

Activity 1

In class, analyse the students' most popular qualities in their 'spouse wanted' advertisements. Ensure that these include true friendship, loyalty, being understanding, and all the other virtues presented in this chapter.

Activity 2

Present a few of the accounts of perseverance to the class, and ask students to comment on them. Emphasise the rewards of perseverance.

Activity 3

In class analyse the best answers from each group. Mention that the most significant aspects in any ceremony emphasise a new starting point or else a reward for an activity in someone's life. Establish a connection between that type of ceremony and the start of a shared life of marriage.

Specific Resolutions

To 'see through' film and story depictions of love and marriage that end with a declaration of love or a wedding scene, and to realise that good marriages are built gradually.

To 'see through' negative social myths about marriage.

To build up their own character strengths of loyalty, perseverance, kindness, supportiveness, etc.

Chapter 18
The Power of One

General Information

Topic

The virtues needed to form a happy family.

Content

▶ Taking initiative: the power of one.

▶ Small kindnesses count: the power of one.

▶ Family relationships are a permanent support system.

Objectives

Knowing
▶ Understanding the essential characteristics and features of a happy family.

▶ To notice messages about family life that surround us and choose the best ones.

Accepting
▶ To reject distorted ideas of family life and accept responsibility for personal contributions.

Doing .
▶ To contribute to a happier family by virtuous living.

Areas of Human Development to be Emphasised

▶ Group maturity: in the family.

Class Plan

1 Knowing

Motivation
Ask students about the people in their family—the numbers, ages, and sexes.

Story context
Alice confides in Charlie that her family is going through a hard time.

Introduction
If family members act kindly and considerately even during difficulties, they will become closer and happier.

Presentation
Key Ideas

- The family is a support system.

- Virtues are needed for living in community.

- Family relationships are important.

Topic Development

A   Taking initiative—the power of one

The chapter title refers both to the power of one person, and that of one daily kindness.

Stephen Covey, author of *The Seven Habits of Highly Effective Families*, urges people to be 'proactive' in their families—to take individual responsibility to make things more pleasant. One person can make a difference. One optimistic, positive, helpful, peaceful person can relieve a difficult family atmosphere. All family members put things into the family 'pot' and should be concerned about the quality of their contributions.

B   Small kindnesses count

Tell the students the following story:

A sixth-former, John, was chosen to give a Prize Day speech because of his high academic achievements. He related how his first days at the school had been very hard. One day he dropped all his books. This was the last straw. Yet a helpful student bent down and picked them up, stacking them nearly, gathering the scattered papers, etc. John said that he had been planning to go home that night and commit suicide. But the student's kindness in helping him pick up the books made him think again. In fact, it gave him the hope to change his life, and to achieve happiness and success.

One small act of kindness saved a life! Think of how many small acts of kindness practiced in a home can make life better for everyone.

C   Family relationships are a permanent support system

Friends come and go, but one's family is permanent. We can't divorce our parents or siblings! Even if we could, we would still be related to them and affected by them in many subtle ways. So it is best for us to make the relationships as good as we can! Family members are a built-in support system. They offer companionship, help with all the tasks of daily living, share economically, make money go further, and watch one another's health. They help each other when there is illness or injury, and provide emotional support. So they should be appreciated, and the relationships nurtured.

2   Accepting

Guided Work

Activity 1

Ask students to draw a big pot and imagine this is the family 'pot'. Ask them to write on the pot the family contributions they make, and label them negative or positive. Chores, money from a small job, good jokes, good marks are examples of good contributions.

Complaints, arguments, demands are negative examples. Does the family 'stew' taste bitter or nourishing? How can they change their contributions to make it better?

Activity 2

Ask students to look at Activity 18 in their Book (p.224) and find the examples:

Activity 18

Where in the story in Chapter 18 can you find these virtues [needed for family life]?

Kindness

Understanding

Trust

Self-sacrifice

Helping others

Consideration

Hope

Belief that things can change

Belief in each other's goodness

Responsibility

Duty

Commitment

3   Doing

Evaluation

Activity 1

Share ideas for an ideal 'pot' but let in some typical 'negative' contributions. Emphasise that students should strive to be part of the solution in their families. Note the quote, "If you're not part of the solution, you're part of the problem."

Activity 2

Discuss the virtues mentioned, in context, ensuring that students understand these.

Specific Resolution

To take individual responsibility in family/group relations to be a positive force.

Chapter 19
Dad's Promise

General Information

Topic

Relationships in the family.

Content

▸ Families are started and sustained by love and promises.

▸ Family first.

▸ Resolving conflict.

▸ Don't compare families.

Objectives

Knowing

▸ The history of every family begins with the love of two people.

▸ Love is the basis and nourishment of families.

▸ Learning how to react to friction in the family.

Accepting

▸ Rejecting derogatory opinions about one's own family.

▸ Being ready to resolve conflicts within the family.

▸ Accepting the importance of faithfulness.

Doing

▸ Living by the virtues that foster closeness within a family.

▸ Seeing one's own family realistically and objectively.

Areas of Human Development to be Emphasised

▸ Development of virtues.

▸ Family dynamics.

Class Plan

1 Knowing

Motivation

Ask students to consider the importance of promises,and discuss the effects of broken and kept promises.

Story context:

Charlie's dad has promised to take Louis to a game, but clash of commitments brings family conflict.

Introduction

A broken promise causes family strife.

Presentation

Key Ideas

▶   Families are built on love.

▶   Faithfulness sustains family love.

▶   Each family is unique.

Topic Development

A   Families are started and sustained by love, and kept promises

In this story Charlie's father breaks a promise, which leads to pain and family conflict. Emphasise that broken promises are so called because something actually is 'broken' between people, and it hurts. Sometimes promises cannot be kept, but it is important that the person breaking the promise make amends for the pain caused.

Charlie's mother gently reminds his father that a broken promise hurts. She also reminds him that wherever possible he keeps his promises to her and this strengthens their marriage and family life. She supports him further by not letting Charlie criticise him behind his back, and by helping him decide what he should do now.

All promises are important, and keeping them is a form of faithfulness that supports and sustains relationships of love.

B   Family first

As pointed out earlier, family relationships are primary—i.e. first—relationships. Many families suffer because the members don't give the family enough importance—they are more concerned with other things. This may be unavoidable if the parents are compelled to work long hours, but there is always some choice and control.

For instance, a Nielsen study in 1996 indicated that the average child in the United States spent thirty-five hours per week watching television as opposed to thirty-five minutes of meaningful conversation with parents. How can children inherit their parents' wisdom and experience without spending more time together? It is important to invest time and energy into family relationships, and students can be a part of this.

In Charlie's family, the work meeting causing his dad to break his promise is optional, and, supported by his family, he is able to say no to his boss. His wife plants the idea:

"You think I should tell my boss I can't come to a business meeting?"

"Maybe, if the meeting isn't that important. It's important to keep your promises to the children. You always try to keep your promises to me."

Things turn out well for the father, and his standing with his boss is enhanced.

"Well, what did he say?" everyone wanted to know.

"He's a family man too and he knows that it's important to keep commitments." Dad looked relieved and pleased.

People who keep to their family commitments are respected.

C   Resolving conflict

Point out that when Charlie inadvertently aggravates his brother's and father's conflict, he bows out so that at least he is not part of the problem.

He flopped down on the couch in the living room. "Can I turn on the TV now or are you two going to keep arguing all night?"

"Watch that attitude, young man!" said Dad sharply.

Charlie sighed. He apologised and went into the kitchen.

Charlie's mother stays calm, so she does not become part of the problem. Although she thinks the father should keep his promise, she persuades him gently and in private.

The father and Louis reconnect in a pillow fight after the father has decided what to do, and tension is released.

"Don't suffocate yourself, son," said Dad, trying to pull the pillow away. Louis resisted him, which started a playful wrestling match—Louis trying his hardest to keep the pillow and Dad trying to get it away from him.

Eventually, Louis surrendered the pillow. "Honest, Dad?" he asked.

"Honest," said Dad, looking at Mum. "I like to keep my promises."

…The living room, which had been the scene of so much arguing, was now where Louis and Dad sat down to apologise and forgive each other. Then they settled back to watch TV together, Dad's arm along the back of the sofa behind Louis.

D   Don't compare families

Each family is unique, each has its own unique dynamics, struggles and strong points. Another family may look happier or less happy than ours, but we cannot know what it is like actually to be a part of that family. So, to nurture good family relationships, it is best not to compare our situation or our family members with other people's families.

Charlie's chides his brother on this point when he compares their father to Joey's dad:

"Look at Joey's dad. He takes him to movies and football matches—and he buys him all the latest video games!"

"But Joey's dad only sees him at weekends! His parents are divorced. Yeah, all he does is treat him, but how many times has Joey said he wished his dad was around all week and not just at weekends?"

"Hmm. But his dad is cool."

"Yeah, well, maybe he is. But you can't compare our situation to Joey's or anyone else's, or theirs to ours, because you don't know the whole story. Let's just appreciate what we have."

2   Accepting

Guided Work

Activity 1

Ask students to take the promise-keeping test in Activity 19 in their Book (p.225):

Activity 19

How good are you at keeping promises?

1.   Your third-best friend asks you to go bowling. You've got nothing to do, so you agree. Then your best friend asks you to go to a cool movie at the same time. Do you:

   a.   Call your third-best friend and say you are sick.

   b.   Call your third-best friend and say something has come up and you can't go Friday night.

   c.   Tell your best friend that you'd love to go, but that you've already promised to do something with someone else that evening.

2.   Your teacher is staying late, and you have told her that you will go home and fetch your comprehension test. When you get home, though, your favourite TV programme is on. Time ticks away until it is almost too late to get back to school with your test. You:

   a.   Call the teacher and tell her your mum won't let you walk back to school.

   b.   Run to the school as fast as you can.

   c.   Call the teacher and apologise and accept the consequences.

3.   You said you would clean your room before going to the park. You put it off, though, and now your friend is at the door, ready to go to the park. You:

   a.   Tell your friend you need to clean your room.

   b.   Figure you'll do it quickly after the park, before your Mum sees it.

   c.   Think your Mum will understand why you put it off.

Activity 2

Discuss: what do students think of Charlie in this story? His dad? His mum? Louis?

3 Doing

Evaluation

Activity 1

Discuss the results of the promise-keeping test. On the board, write these scores:

Question 1: Answer a: 0; Answer b: 1; Answer c: 2

Question 2: Answer a: 0; Answer b: 1; Answer c: 2

Question 3: Answer a: 2; Answer b: 1; Answer c: 0

5-6: You are pretty good at keeping promises. Sometimes you find it difficult, but you do try.

3-4: You try to twist things to your own advantage. Remember that keeping promises sometimes means self-sacrifice.

0-2: You need to work on being more honest with yourself and others; otherwise people are going to stop trusting you.

Emphasise the importance of being part of the solution, not part of the problem, in a family. Ways to do this include showing faithfulness and loyalty, and keeping promises.

Activity 2

Make sure this analysis helps students understand each person's position in these circumstances:

▶ the father's difficulty in making a decision when work is involved.

▶ the mother's trying to show fairness in all circumstances.

▶ Charlie's trying not to interfere.

▶ Louis' anger in the beginning and his forgiveness at the end.

Specific Resolution

To develop the virtue of faithfulness by practising keeping promises now.

Chapter 20
The Family

General Information

Topic

The family in society and history.

Content

▶ The family in history.
▶ The family and society.
▶ The importance of the family.

Objectives

Knowing

▶ Understanding the role of the family in history and society.
▶ Identifying the salient features of the family throughout history and to recognising the importance of one's own family—now and in future.

Accepting

▶ Valuing the family as the basic unit of society.

Doing

▶ Respecting one's family and acting so as to help it grow and function better.

Areas of Human Development to be Emphasised

▶ Group maturity: the family and society.

Class Plan

1   Knowing

Motivation
In international polls of things people value most, 'family' is always no.1 or no.2.

Story context:
A research project on the family brings Alan, Charlie, Marianne, Alice, Ben and Sara together as a team.

Introduction
Charlie and his classmates discover the importance of family through a research project.

Presentation
Key Ideas
▶   The family is the building block of community and society.
▶   The family has figured prominently in history.
▶   The family contributes to peace on many levels.

Topic Development

A   The family in history

The students learn that the family is the natural, basic nucleus of society. From earliest times the family has afforded protection and means of progress. It has been important in history for peacemaking between warring nations (see the example about Alexander the Great).

Families are also important now. When young children live surrounded by their parents' love, they become peaceful adults who elect peaceful rulers; sometimes they are elected themselves and use their authority to create a peaceful environment.

Explain the differences between a truce (the mere absence of fights) and peace, which is an inner and total attitude related to respect, justice, solidarity, and altruism. This type of peace stems from peaceful families.

B   The family and society

The family is an important economic unit as even young family members can contribute to tasks of feeding and clothing the family. Family members can cooperate in the division of work in the best interests of the whole family, and families can work together in creating and sharing resources: community watch schemes, babysitting circles, for example.

Families cut down on crime as they provide a healthy structure for male energies, and they raise people who are used to relating well with others in community.

Those with a good, loving relationship with grandparents and a loving understanding of old people will find it easier to be polite to a less well known elderly neighbour. Relating well with sisters or brothers makes it easier to relate to other girls or boys at school, and to others in society.

C   **The importance of father and mother within the family**

Sara pinpoints the importance of both parents to the family:

"You know, I think we're missing something. We've said a lot about women, and the pressure on them to do a good job out at work and in the family, and we've said that both parents are needed to provide a stable background. But what Marianne says makes me think we need to put it more simply than that. Isn't this what it comes down to: if the man isn't completely tied in with his own children, the children he has fathered himself, then those children suffer. That's an incredibly important fact and I actually think it's a very positive one."

Any family arrangement not based on the marriage of the parents usually removes the father from the close family unit. This matters both to him and the children. Marriage is the only guarantee that his rights as father will be fully recognised: this is why marriage should be considered as important to the man as to the woman. This harks back to Chapter 17 where Mrs Alam points out that wearing white symbolises the bride's sexual purity and that her children will belong to the marriage and to her new husband.

Charlie learns how important a stable family is by reading that family breakdown contributes to crime, delinquency, poverty and unemployment. Thus, marrying the right person and being a good spouse oneself is so vital because it also affects society.

2   Accepting

Guided Work

Activity 1

Ask students, in groups, to discuss and list some functions and uses of the family.

3   Doing

Evaluation

Activity 1

Ask each group to present their conclusions about the role of the family. Ask students if they gained in understanding and appreciating the importance of their family and all families.

Point out that the simplest, most everyday things, such as water and the family, have so many uses and functions and are found everywhere, so that we take them for granted and forget how important they are.

Specific Resolutions

To take family life—present and future—more seriously.

To treat the family as central to human existence.

Chapter 21
Faithful Friend

General Information

Topic

Fidelity as the basis of all friendships.

Content

▶ The importance of fidelity.

▶ Dealing with pain.

▶ Fidelity in friendship gives practice for fidelity in marriage.

Objectives

Knowing
▶ Understanding fidelity and its characteristics.

▶ Relating fidelity to good friendships and relationships.

Accepting
▶ Rejecting infidelity and disloyalty, as they destroy relationships.

Doing
▶ Reflecting on personal experience of fidelity in friendships.

Areas of Human Development to be Emphasised

▶ Developing character strength.

▶ Developing the virtue of fidelity.

Class Plan

1   Knowing

Motivation

Ask students to reflect whether they have been in a situation similar to Alice's in the story and whether they could sympathise with her.

Story context:

A girl Alice considered a good friend does not invite her to a party. Alice and Charlie learn about loyal and disloyal friends.

Introduction

Fidelity is crucial in good relationships, from friendships to marriage.

Presentation

Key Ideas

▸   Disloyalty causes great pain.

▸   True friends are faithful.

▸   Good spouses are faithful.

Topic Development

A   The importance of fidelity

Almost everyone has experienced being left out or let down by people they trusted as friends. It is always painful, but is almost always a learning experience too. Also, all of us have let down other people at some point. This lesson aims to show students that all personal relationships call upon our steadfastness if they are to flourish. Fidelity keeps the heart solid, unbroken, and able to respond well to friendship and love.

Erik Erikson said that, in developmental terms, fidelity was the primary virtue or character strength to be developed in adolescence and was fundamental to success in future life stages. It helps develop intimacy, something he considers as the opposite of isolation. This lesson begins to prepare students to develop this crucial virtue.

B   Dealing with pain

Since painful situations occur, it is important for students to have perspective ('every cloud has a silver lining') as well as boundaries regarding friendship. They must learn to endure the inevitable blows in relationships. While it is good to be open and trusting, they also need to be discerning and exercise wise judgment when choosing friends.

One way for them to build perspective is through the ancient Taoist story of a man who lost his horse. Various versions of this story exist in China and in the Middle East, but the same basic message. Ask students to read this text in their Books (p.226):

Support Activity 21

> Good luck? Bad luck? Who knows? Have you ever found that what looked like bad luck wasn't, after all?
>
> There was once a wise man in ancient China. He was poor, but he had a beautiful horse. Everyone admired his horse and said he was fortunate to have it. One night, the horse ran away. Oh, how unfortunate, everyone said. Not necessarily, the wise man thought—let's see.
>
> In fact, the next day the horse came back with a whole stable-full of horses, all as beautiful and strong as he was.
>
> Everyone said that this was great good fortune, but the wise man kept an open mind. His wisdom showed when his son broke his leg after falling off one of the horses as he was riding.
>
> Everyone said that this was terribly bad luck, but the wise man said it might not be so unlucky after all. In fact, war came to China and all the young men went off to fight and died, except the wise man's son, who was excused because of his broken leg.

The story's moral, of course, is that what seems like painfully bad luck may be the opposite. Alice in fact gains much from the 'bad fortune' of not being invited to Gloria's party. She has a special evening with her parents, benefits from their support, and her friendship with loyal Tiffany is made even stronger. Both she and her cousin Charlie learn the importance of fidelity, and discernment about friends and future spouses. If Alice had had the 'good fortune' of an invitation to Gloria's party, she would have missed out on all those valuable things.

By taking a longer view and realising that what appears to be good or bad may not necessarily turn out so, students gain wisdom and perspective to bear life's knocks.

C Fidelity in friendship is practice for marriage

If students can relate to Alice's pain about the party, they should get some idea of the much greater pain that many people carry around with them because of broken relationships of all kinds. As Alice's mother says:

"Betrayal hurts, doesn't it? And you will find in life that the closer you are to a person the worse the pain. There are many people who carry that sort of hurt inside them. That's why it is so important to be kind to everyone—even when they don't seem to want it."

In fact, therapists have vividly described infidelity (sexual) in marriage as causing 'a volcano of pain'[10]. Remind students that when people make vows to one another, there is expectation and trust. To violate that is to break another person's heart and cause tremendous internal pain.

Fidelity builds trust, which allows people to open their hearts to one another more fully. Tiffany and Alice find their friendship strengthened because of fidelity. They will enjoy each other more and more as trust continues to grow between them.

---

10.   cf. Dr. Don Lusterman as quoted in : Subotnik, Rona and Harris, Gloria G. *Surviving Infidelity: Making Decisions, Recovering from the Pain.* 3rd Edition. Holbrook, MA: Adams Media, 2005. ISBN 1593374801 p. 188.

The same is true in marriage, where opening the heart and revealing one's most tender and vulnerable self are the journey and the goal. Trust, built on fidelity, becomes a safe ground where two hearts meet and experience the joys of love together.

2 Accepting

Guided Work

Activity 1

Ask students to reflect that almost everyone has been 'dumped' at some time, and most of us have been guilty of doing this. You could ask them to write briefly about times when they were left out by someone they wanted to be with, and also about times when they may have left others out.

Activity 2

Ask students to re-read the story of Penelope and Ulysses from their texts. Then ask them, in groups, to discuss it and draw at least two lessons from it.

3 Doing

Evaluation

Activity 1

In class, comment on the reflections the students come up with. Draw conclusions which establish parallels with the chapter's content.

It is not possible to change the behaviour of others, but each should re-examine personal relationships, thinking of ways to be kinder and more inclusive of others. Practising loyalty and kindness now will help improve all relationships and be good practice for marriage.

Activity 2

Discuss in class the groups' conclusions about the story. Emphasise the virtues of fidelity, patience, and perseverance.

Specific Resolutions

To practice being faithful to friends and family.

To grow strong in fidelity in preparation for a happy, stable marriage later in life.

Chapter 22
Dreams and Schemes: Looking at the Future

General Information

Topic

Visualising the future with idealism and realism.

Content

▸   The need to have a vision for the future.
▸   The need to be both realistic and idealistic about the future.

Objectives

Knowing
▸   To understand what a realistic vision of the future is.

Accepting
▸   Having a realistic basis for future plans and hopes.

Doing
▸   To maintain ideals, but realistically.

Areas of Human Development to be Emphasised

▸   Seeing in perspective.
▸   Goal-setting.

Class Plan

1   Knowing

Motivation

Start discussion and interest by asking: What do you want to be when you grow up?

Story context:

Charlie, Alice, Ron, Ben, and Marianne are dreaming of their future. Charlie decides to ask his 'Grandpa' for advice on what he should be when he grows up.

Introduction

Sorting goals from unrealistic dreams takes thoughtful discernment and good advice.

Presentation

Key Ideas

▶   Dreams are beautiful and necessary, but must be tempered with realism.

▶   Different jobs suit different people: it is how we do them that counts.

▶   The future will just happen randomly to those without plans and goals.

Topic Development

A   The need to have a vision for the future

It is natural to dream of the future, hoping it will be better than today. Without such 'dreams and schemes' the future is likely just to happen to us, and we may not like it.

Family businesses which were passed on through the generations were common in the past but are less so now, so that more students have to make their own decisions on their future.

During a slack period, Charlie asked Mr Travis, "What made you decide to go into the grocery business?"

"Oh," he said, "I didn't have much choice. I was brought up helping out in the shop and it was always assumed that I would take over the family business. This was my father's shop, you know. Very proud of it, he was, and rightly, too. He began from nothing—and look what he built up!"

Mr Travis points out the advantages in having a way of life ready carved out. Charlie is not in this position, and Mr Travis suggests that he should dream high, stretch himself, but also be realistic. Charlie knows he does not want to work all his life in a grocery shop.

Ron says his father had said: *"Most people end up doing a boring job just to make ends meet."*

Charlie comments that a job one person finds boring another enjoys. The important thing is matching job to person and doing it well:

"The other [postman] always has a big smile on his face. He says hello to everyone and still gets the post delivered on time. It seems to me that the important thing is to find the job that suits you."

Emphasise that the people Ron's father described as dissatisfied did not think ahead when they were young. The more that character and talents are developed in childhood, the more possibilities will be open later on.

B   The need to be both realistic and idealistic about the future

Having goals and dreams is not enough to achieve happiness and satisfaction in life, though. The dreams must have some chance of fulfillment, and the goals be realistic: people have to work hard to achieve what they wish.

The story shows the process of sorting out realistic dreams. The children remember some of the dreams they had when they were younger, but have since rejected.

"Remember when we wanted to be train drivers?" [Ben] asked. "We thought it would be such fun to control a big engine and wear a smart uniform."

…"How about being a rock star?" said Ron, plucking imaginary guitar strings.

"I think you have to be able to sing, Ron," observed Marianne.

"Oh, come on... Let me dream."

"How about you, Alice?" asked Charlie. "You used to want to be a film star, didn't you?"

"Well, I did," Alice replied. She considered a moment. "I used to think it would be cool to see myself on the big screen wearing gorgeous clothes and riding in fast cars. And I like acting. But it must be hard being a star— so many of them seem to end up on drink or drugs, and they often don't seem to have much of a family life.It would be great to be a film star if I could be a success in my private life, too, but I don't think I'm tough enough."

Charlie expresses realism about being an Olympic gold medallist, something he dreams of every time he watches the Olympics on TV:

"Most of those people started working on their sport when they were only eight or nine. I'm already too late."

So how does a person go about making realistic goals? Alice says, *"I guess you've got to work out what you'd like to do and what you're good at."* Charlie decides to turn to his 'Grandpa' for advice.

'Grandpa' expresses a great deal of idealism about planning for the future. He says:

"The most important thing… is to be a good man, a good husband, a good father, and a good neighbour. I think that is true success. It's easy to think the measure of a man is his income or how much property he has or what his job title is, but that just is not true. I don't think what kind of job or career you have matters as much as doing it honestly and well and for the right reasons…the most important thing about anything you do in life is that you do it to help and benefit others. That way you can't fail."

Grandpa mixes idealism in his advice on choosing a specific dream:

"[It's] the thing you can't stop doing—the thing you do for free, the thing you do in your spare time, the thing you love…"

Yet he also gives realistic and practical advice:

"Pay attention to what you are especially good at. That may be your gift… it should be something you are already showing promise in." He also says, "[It] should be something you have to try hard for. You should aim high, but it must also be something possible, not just a crazy pipe dream." He adds this hard-headed wisdom: "Don't imagine that, because you have a talent for it, you don't have to work hard at it."

Emphasise to students that the subjects they enjoy at school may give them a clue as to where there future strengths lie. Maths, science, history, language, are all useful training for the mind in their own right and lead on to university and college courses which open up interesting careers. Further academic education doesn't suit everybody and those with a more practical turn of mind should be encouraged to get good training and work experience in their chosen fields.

Their extracurricular activities (art, music, sports, school newspapers, etc) may also help them in their choices. What helps nobody is to waste time e.g. in front of a television, expecting a good job just to appear.

2   Accepting

Guided Work

Activity 1

Ask students to imagine getting on a bus, wanting to go to a city centre theatre, and asking the driver, "Does this bus go to the city centre?" The driver says, "I really don't know where the bus is going. I just drive and we end up where we end up." Then, ask them to consider the following questions:

▸   Is that any way to run a bus company?

▸   Is that any way to run a life?

You need a clear idea of where you want to go in order to get there.

Activity 2

Goals are dreams with deadlines. To make a dream come true, it should be broken down into what needs to be done on the practical level to draw nearer to its realisation.

Ask students to make a list of their dreams for the future. Decide, perhaps with the help of an adult, which ones are realistic and which aren't. Tell them not to aim too low, but not to try to achieve the impossible either.

Focus the activity by asking students to do Activity 22 in their Books (p.226).

Activity 22

> **Situation A:** Every time Jenny watched figure skating on TV, she wanted to be an Olympic figure skater. But Jenny was already 15 and she had never skated before! Given that most Olympic stars have been practising since they were much younger than 15 and that Jenny had no gift for skating, was her dream realistic?
>
> **Situation B:** Jamie wanted to be a lawyer. He loved the idea of making sure justice was done. His teachers said he had great comprehension and speaking skills and a real eye for detail. He found out about scholarships and tried to get the necessary grades. He went to a local firm of solicitors and asked what he needed to do. He got a part-time job to save up for law school. Given Jamie's talents, his strong desire, and his willingness, do you think his is a realistic dream?

Activity 3 (optional or for another moment)

Teachers might want to consider having a Career Day when they invite people of different professions to come in and talk to the students about what they do, how they came to be doing it, and how to prepare for this career.

3 Doing

Evaluation

Activity 1

Comment with the class on their conclusions about the bus company. Point out that there must be a clear destination and goal to avoid aimless activity.

Activity 2

Talk about the examples in the exercise, and then about some goals and dreams that students may want to share. Try to provide examples that show the difference between realistic and unrealistic goals. Ask students why it is important to have dreams and goals, and ask them what they seem to be gifted in. Ask whether they have any new ideas about what they want to be when they grow up as a result of this lesson.

Specific Resolutions

To set goals for the future which are both realistic and idealistic.

To list and take age-appropriate steps toward these goals.

**Unit V:
Changes in My Life—Puberty**

Abilities:
*To understand that the changes in puberty affect the whole being, physical, psychological, social and spiritual;
*To respect privacy;
*To realise that poor communication leads to misunderstanding;
*To learn that swings of mood are normal and to develop patience with self and others.
Number of Chapters: 8 (23 to 30)

Chapter 23
Going through Changes

General Information

Topic

Respecting the bodily changes of early puberty.

Content

- The hormonal basis of physical changes and the changes themselves.
- The purpose of these changes is parenthood—a great gift.
- Respect.

Objectives

Knowing
- Understanding the changes taking place in the bodies of adolescents.
- Realising that these changes prepare them for motherhood and fatherhood.

Accepting
- Happily and respectfully accepting the bodily changes taking place.
- Respecting others who develop at different paces.

Doing
- Noticing and understanding the changes taking place in one's own body.

Areas of Human Development to be Emphasised

> ▶ Growth and development.

Class Plan

1 Knowing

Motivation

Explain that this story focuses on bodily changes associated with sexual maturation and so may cause students some embarrassment. Emphasise that these are all natural changes and should be treated with calm, respect, and dignity.

Story context:

Charlie and Alice are beginning to experience the changes puberty brings.

Introduction

Puberty brings about many changes, which require understanding.

Presentation

Key Ideas

> ▶ Puberty is preparation for future parenthood.
> ▶ Respect for oneself and others is essential during this transitional time.

Topic Development

A   The hormonal basis of physical changes and the changes themselves

Define a hormone as a natural body chemical. Explain that around their age the pituitary gland, a little gland under the brain, starts sending hormones to the rest of the body to urge it to begin growing toward sexual maturity and adulthood.

Specific hormones and their effects and functions are discussed further in Chapter 26. Specific hormones are also discussed in Chapter 30 of Year 7, 'Just Right'. The information is reproduced here (Alice and her friend Alisha are discussing hormones):

Oestrogen and progesterone, which told the womb to form a 'nest' for a baby—that was OK. They sounded pretty much like what they were-natural body chemicals. But the others sounded quite frightening. There was gonadotropin-releasing hormone, which stimulated the pituitary gland to release yet more hormones-luteinizing hormone and follicle-stimulating hormone. They went to the various parts of the male and female body, telling them to mature. Alice thought they must be easier to live with than they were to pronounce.

Write on the board these hormone names and their functions as described in the story.

Mention specific changes that boys and girls, like Charlie and Alice, will experience.

For boys: voice changes, increase in bodily hair, enlargement in the genital area, height and weight increases, moodiness, fatigue.

For girls: breast development, broadening of hips, menstruation, moodiness, height and weight increases, fatigue.

B   The purpose of these changes is parenthood–a great gift

Mention that these changes are taking place with a goal in mind: parenthood.

"Alice's body and the bodies of the girls in your class are preparing for future motherhood… But, like everything else in nature, that doesn't happen all at once. It's gradual. Alice's breasts are developing so that, when she has babies, she can give them milk. She may be putting on a little weight around her hips too, as they get broader to cradle a baby in her womb…Alice will begin what is called 'menstruating' every month, if she hasn't already. Her womb will prepare a soft setting of tissue for a baby to grow in. If the egg is not fertilised within three days, then the tissue will break down and be discharged from the body."

There are more details in Chapter 26 about boys' bodies, but Charlie's dad sums it up: *"Your body is working very hard to turn you from a boy into a man."* An important part of manhood is being a father.

The changes students are experiencing are following a natural blueprint for physical and sexual maturity. All they need to do is let nature take its course and adopt an attitude of self-respect and respect for others as they undergo these changes. Sexual maturity and parenthood are free gifts—but never to be treated cheaply.

C   Respect

Explain that sexual maturity and parenthood are awesome, powerful things, involving new life and our deepest emotions. Subsequent chapters discuss respecting their own sexuality and that of others; Year 9 deals with it in detail. For now point out that the changes they are undergoing are signs of adulthood and require great respect.

They should not tease, laugh at or draw undue attention to one another's maturation processes. The most uncomfortable aspects of adolescence are temporary and will pass. They may feel out-of-proportion themselves or out-of-proportion in relationship to others, but eventually everyone will be well within the normal range for adults. They simply need to accept and respect the processes in themselves and others.

2   Accepting

Guided Work

Activity 1

Ask students to tackle mentally Activity 23 in their Books (p.227). They could note physical and emotional changes in separate columns.

Activity 23

> Have you noticed any of the signs of puberty Alice and Charlie are experiencing in this chapter in yourself? Do you feel the same way they did about those changes? Reflect on similarities and differences, drawing a Venn diagram between yourself and Charlie for boys, and yourself and Alice for girls. You might draw one for physical similarities and differences, and one for emotional similarities and differences. (This is for your eyes only!)

Activity 2

Have a class discussion on the meaning of 'respect'. First decide on a good definition, and then some behaviours that show respect.

3   Doing

Evaluation

Activity 1

Sum up the many changes they are undergoing, and the need to treat themselves and others with patience. Ask volunteers to share ideas for an ideal diagram.

Activity 2

Encourage everyone's participation in the discussion, and try to draw clear conclusions about self-respect and respect for others.

Specific Resolutions

To treat self and others with the respect proper to the awesome bodily changes they are experiencing.

Chapter 24
Privacy, Please!

General Information

Topic

Respecting privacy.

Content

▶ The need for privacy.

▶ Parents as allies in building and respecting privacy.

▶ Respecting the privacy of others and commanding respect for one's own.

Objectives

Knowing

▶ Understanding the importance and implications of privacy.

▶ Realising that parents can help build and protect privacy.

Accepting

▶ Valuing privacy.

Doing

▶ Respecting and protecting personal privacy.

▶ Showing a positive and open attitude toward parents.

Areas of Human Development to be Emphasised

▶ Modesty.

▶ Personal management.

" Group maturity.

Class Plan

1   Knowing

Motivation
Ask students whether they keep a diary. Suggest they start doing so.

Story context:

Charlie is feeling an increasing need for privacy now that he is entering puberty. His mother helps him gain some physical and spiritual privacy, but his younger sister and classmate Alan intrude.

Introduction
Privacy should be respected: it is precious and necessary.

Presentation
Key Ideas
▶   Physically and spiritually we sometimes need privacy for personal growth.

▶   Understanding parents and adults can foster this privacy.

▶   The whole person is precious and deserves respect.

Topic Development

A   The need for privacy

All people sometimes need privacy, especially when growing and developing. Charlie is within his rights in not wanting his younger sister to see his developing body—he feels naturally modest. He also does not want his inmost thoughts and feelings (recorded in his diary) bandied about the school by Alan. Charlie wants a healthy kind of privacy.

Explain to students that our faces are very different, and that our body language reveals our attitudes. On the other hand, the 'private parts' (the genital areas) are much more alike. Modesty (which leads us to cover the most intimate parts of the body) is a natural human tendency. It protects us from being judged by our sexual capacity alone, while ensuring that others get to know our individuality and personality.

Charlie does not demand privacy to hide anything shameful (such as drugs or pornography). His inmost thoughts are not much different from Alan's—but they need to remain personal and private.

The mind, heart, and nervous system sometimes need privacy to be calmed and strengthened, to unfold, to avoid the stress of being on constant view, and to learn about the inner person—particularly in adolescence.

B   Parents as allies in building and respecting privacy

Charlie's mother understands all this intuitively. Although she cannot give Charlie a room to himself—and is not even sure that this would be best for him—she trains his younger sister to knock before entering, and gives Charlie a diary. He finds writing in his diary a great relief. Perhaps this aspect could be taught by asking the students in what ways Charlie's mother supports his need for privacy.

Most parents are very considerate when their children are undergoing physical changes in puberty, and will try hard to provide physical privacy. As long as nothing unhealthy is being concealed, young people can consider their parents good allies in this need.

Teachers too act in *loco parentis*—in a parental role. Mr Murphy is an ally in preserving Charlie's privacy. He compels Alan to return the diary. Mrs Alam is an ally in Alan's privacy because she suggested he keep a journal as a release for his feelings. Adults in general will often defend the privacy of adolescents by preventing others from invading their privacy.

C   Respecting the privacy of others and commanding respect for one's own

When Alan invades Charlie's privacy by stealing and reading his diary, Charlie rebukes him: *"Alan, you took something of mine. You didn't give it back. You lied about it. You totally invaded my privacy. All I can say is, I wouldn't do that to you."*

Charlie's statement shows that he respects Alan's privacy more than Alan respects his. At this point that Alan relents and begins to show more respect for Charlie's privacy. He also reveals some private things about himself: that he is lonely, in need of companionship and understanding:

"I wanted to find out if you thought the same way about things as me."

Charlie reflects that: *the human heart doubles in size during puberty, Mrs Alam had said. And friendships deepen. Could it be that Alan, of all people, was looking to Charlie to be his friend?*

Charlie is well on the way toward respecting his own and others' privacy, and Alan has probably learnt a lesson too.

2   Accepting

Guided Work

Activity 1

Ask students to read Activity 24 in their Books (p.227).

Activity 24

> Keeping a diary or journal is a wonderful way to keep track of the changes you are going through day by day and month by month, and to articulate your feelings about them. It is useful for self-reflection. Sometimes, in writing, things come out more clearly, and you understand yourself better.

Make time in class each day for students to write in their journals.

An excellent book on bodily privacy is Wendy Shalit's *A Return to Modesty*[11]. Students may be interested in some excerpts and points from this book. Shalit comments that the lack of modesty and privacy experienced in many settings is causing a high level of stress among young women, who feel a constant sexual pressure. Statistics reveal that this pressure, without any commitment on the part of young men, ends up undermining women's personalities and happiness.

---

11.   Shalit, Wendy. *A Return to Modesty: Discovering the Lost Virtue.* Tappan, NJ: Touchstone, 2000. ISBN 0684863170.

Activity 2

Too much openness about the body does not relax people; it actually tenses them up. Modesty allows people to relate more naturally without constantly being distracted by sexuality.

This may be illustrated by asking some students to stand up and give an impromptu speech about a topic they draw from a hat. Then ask them to give another impromptu speech, but this time from behind a desk or box where they are hidden. Ask them to compare the two experiences: was it easier to speak to others when not being viewed?

3   Doing

Evaluation

Activity 1

Discuss with the class the benefits of keeping a diary. If some students already do so, this is a good opportunity for them to share their experience with the rest of the class.

Emphasise the importance of respecting someone else's diary.

Activity 2

Ask the students who stood in front of the class to comment on the differences they felt about the two situations.

Emphasise the inhibitions they may have felt when they stood in front of an audience.

Then make comparison between speaking and doing more 'intimate' things. The contrast will help them to understand the need for respect.

Emphasise the need to respect each person's dignity—both physically and spiritually.

Specific Resolutions

To show greater respect for the need for physical and spiritual modesty and privacy—one's own and others'; to encourage others to do likewise.

To discourage—in oneself and others—any 'peeping' at the opposite sex or at one another, any teasing about the body or prying into others' private worlds.

Chapter 25
Invasion of Privacy

General Information

Topic

Respecting the opposite sex.

Content

▶ Calmly and respectfully accepting changes in the opposite sex.
▶ Never showing disrespect to the opposite sex.
▶ The importance of personal boundaries.

Objectives

Knowing
▶ Recognising the increasing need for privacy of the opposite sex—who are also growing and developing.

Accepting
▶ Avoiding disrespect of the privacy of others.
▶ Being patient with others who feel insecure at the changes they are experiencing.

Doing
▶ Being natural and straightforward in dealings with those of the opposite sex.

Areas of Human Development to be Emphasised

▶ Establishing personal boundaries.

Class Plan

1   Knowing

Motivation

Explain that violations of other people's 'space' are always serious, threatening, and can affect either sex. For instance, ask boys to imagine an older boy, bigger and stronger, leaning close to them and making threatening remarks. Ask girls to imagine the fear of being alone in a lift with a strong man looking at them oddly.

Story context:

Mary wears tight clothes and draws a lot of attention to her body. When two older pupils assault her in the street, Alice and Charlie come to her rescue. Mary doesn't understand why she is the target of sexual comments. Alice and Charlie show her that she is giving the wrong signals, making men think she is inviting this type of attention.

Introduction

Some pupils in Charlie's and Alice's school are handling puberty development poorly.

Presentation

Key Ideas

▸   It is a tough challenge to deal with the changes puberty brings in oneself and others.

▸   Disrespect for oneself or others makes it all the harder.

Topic Development

A   Accepting changes in the opposite sex with equanimity and respect

Fortunately, most students show reasonable acceptance and respect in dealing with changes in their own bodies. But stress that it is a difficult issue for everyone.

Emphasise that it helps others cope with the changes if we do not advertise them (as Mary did) or draw attention to them with inaccurate, disrespectful names or words.

Charlie thinks that Mary needs to be told to dress more appropriately and urges Alice to tell her. Alice tries to duck out but realises that she is going to have to do something if the teasing, which is now spreading to other girls too, is to stop. How many girls—or boys—would easily manage this task?

Alice and Charlie respect Mary in spite of her actions, although recognising that she is at fault: *"But I don't think she should dress like that. How can they respect her if she doesn't seem to respect herself?"*

They treat Mary with care and respect after the boys attack her. Ask students to name examples of their respect. (Desirable answers: giving her the hanky and the jacket, asking if she is okay, escorting her to the nurse, telling her she has leadership qualities, encouraging her to to dress appropriately.)

B   Rejecting disrespect toward the opposite sex

Both Alice and Charlie feel the boys are wrong to tease Mary and they avoid such disrespect for the opposite sex. They still disapprove of Mary's display of her body, because men may interpret it as a sexual invitation, and they gently tell her so.

124

Alice and Charlie discover that Mary acts as she does because she thinks her body is all she has to offer; she feels she has no value. This lack of self-respect invites men to treat her in a sexually disrespectful way. Alice's and Charlie's compassionate response shows they know this is wrong.

C   The importance of personal boundaries

We are all uncomfortable at intrusion on our personal space. If someone stands or sits too close to us, or touches us when we don't want it, we become very agitated. It is important that we assert these personal boundaries so that others recognise and respect them. (Most people recognise and respect these boundaries instinctively. But the few who do not can be annoying, offensive, and sometimes dangerous.)

Ask students to think about a social situation—perhaps a party at their parents' house. Friends may greet each other with a hug, a kiss, lean on one another's shoulders, etc. But more distant acquaintances keep greater physical distance. They may shake hands on introduction, but little more. Hand-shaking originated long ago, when people would offer one another their open hands to show that they did not have a weapon. It has survived as a traditional sign of trust between newly acquainted strangers.

The degree of intimacy of a relationship is shown by degree of physical closeness. The more distant the relationship, the less physical contact there is. The closer people feel emotionally, the more they touch, brush against each other, lay a hand on one another's shoulders, etc. The physical relationship symbolises the trust between them.

We each have only a few intimates—spouses, immediate family members, relatives, very close friends. Therefore it is important to recognise personal boundaries and assert them if someone seems likely to violate them.

2   Accepting

Guided Work

Activity 1

Ask students, in small groups, to look at Activity 25 (p.227 in their Books), and to discuss how to prevent others from transgressing boundaries, and also what Mary could have done to avoid being attacked.

Activity 25

Enforcing Boundaries

What could Mary have said to the boys the first time they teased her?

1. "Say that again, and I'll go to the Headteacher."

2. "Keep your distance, or I'll report you."

3. "Why don't you grow up?"

Some of these things may seem a little rude, but there is a difference between being rude and being assertive.

Sometimes assertiveness alone can stop someone from crossing the line into our personal boundaries. Being alone with someone of the opposite sex in a dark place is a potentially explosive situation. While Mary defended herself from her aggressors, she could have done more to avoid the problem in the first place.

Activity 2

Ask students, in small groups, to discuss assertive ways to keep others from invading personal boundaries, and role-play them in class.Emphasise that these ways may be subtle. For instance, if a man leans too close to a woman while they are talking, she may calmly step back.

3   Doing

Evaluation
Activity 1

In class, analyse the behaviour of the groups and draw conclusions on ways to enforce respect for personal space. This activity could, if wished, be organised as a contest.

Specific Resolutions

To respect other people's physical boundaries.

To recognise and assert the need for others to respect our own boundaries.

Chapter 26
'Cousins' Talk

General Information

Topic

Hormonal changes during puberty and their influence.

Content

▶ Hormones and what they do.

▶ Coping with the changes.

▶ Care of the pubescent body.

Objectives

Knowing

▶ Knowing the main hormonal changes of puberty and how these affect other changes.

Accepting

▶ Feeling comfortable with the stages of puberty, whenever they happen.

▶ Accepting that the disadvantages felt in puberty will gradually pass.

Doing

▶ Being able to deal with acne, voice change, fatigue, weight change and menstruation.

Areas of Human Development to be Emphasised

▶ Psycho-sexual development.

▶ Personal knowledge and management.

Class Plan

1   Knowing

Motivation

Tell students that this is a very practical chapter providing information on the changes they are experiencing.

Story context:

Charlie reads some factual information about puberty and discusses with Alice how this relates to their daily experiences.

Introduction

Hormones, and their effects in adolescence, are explored.

Presentation

Key Ideas

▶   Proper names of hormones and their functions.

▶   Facts about puberty.

▶   Tips on coping with the bodily changes of puberty.

Topic Development

A   Hormones and what they do

Factual information on hormones can be found by reading through this chapter:

Around our age (although it can happen anywhere between eight and thirteen in girls and ten and fifteen in boys) our brains release a hormone called gonadotropin-releasing hormone, or GnRH for short. Hormones are natural chemicals in the body. When GnRH reaches pituitary gland (you remember, Alice, the 'pit' gland),this gland releases stuff into the bloodstream—in fact, more hormones! It releases luteinising hormone (LH for short), and follicle-stimulating hormone (FSH for short). Boys and girls have both of these hormones in their bodies. These hormones go to work on different parts of the body, depending on whether you're a boy or a girl.

Then describe some of the external manifestations of hormones at work: acne, voice changes in boys, disproportionate hands, feet, limbs, or features, increases in weight and height, cramps and menstruation for girls, spontaneous erections and nocturnal emissions in boys.

Emphasise Charlie's point: *Our bodies are just getting ready for marriage and fathering children.* Emphasise that girls' bodies are also preparing to be wives and mothers. Some of the students may find these changes embarrassing. Reassure them about the negative aspects they may perceive in the growth process and stress positive aspects.

B   Coping with the changes

Parents are the first educators of their children in puberty and this is to be encouraged. You might suggest that the parents of your students read this chapter in the Student Book to make sure that they know what will also be covered in the classroom. Additional information is on our website **www.alivetotheworld.co.uk.** Libraries can also be a useful source of information, as Charlie's parents find. Students should not be encouraged to explore the website on their own since the material that they find could be very inappropriate.

Encourage students to keep turning to trustworthy sources of information and encouragement. Remind them that every single adult has gone through what they are going through, and understands. Charlie and Alice are grateful for their parents' positive supporting attitude, and try themselves have this positive attitude:

"Puberty is a new beginning," he read loudly. "Like when trees start to bud. Everyone has to go through puberty in order to become an adult and have children, just as a tree has to produce blossom before it has fruit."

C   Care of the pubescent body

Remind students of the many tips in the story on caring for themselves at this stage of their lives:

▸   Get enough sleep.

▸   Expect weight and height gain; to make sure it is healthy weight gain, avoid junk foods and fizzy drinks.

▸   Wash with warm water and soap morning and night and use a little spot medication on pimples. Add that it is best to wash with clean hands, not bacteria-ridden facecloths. Warn girls never to sleep with makeup on, as it will clog up the pores, causing oil build-up and pimples! Advise them to replace cosmetics every six months. Bacteria grow in compacts, lipstick cases, on eye shadow and liners.

▸   Exercise for self-esteem, confidence, weight control, and relief of cramps.

▸   Shower daily and after exercise to control sweat, oil, and body odour.

▸   Don't eat sugar, chocolate, or oily foods.

▸   Get calcium from sources other than milk—nuts, seeds, and green leafy vegetables are good sources for this bone- and teeth-strengthening mineral.

▸   Drink plenty of water to control acne, flush out impurities, and aid in the increase in blood volume they are undergoing.

2   Accepting

Guided Work

Activity 1

Ask students to answer the questionnaire in Activity 26 of their Books (p.228):

Activity 26

> From the story, find the correct answers:
>
> 1.   A hormone secreted by the brain that starts the process of puberty is called:
>
>   a.   luteinising hormone
>
>   b.   follicle-stimulating hormone
>
>   c.   gonadotropin-releasing hormone
>
>   d.   testosterone

2. All of the following are characteristics of puberty except:

   a. voice changes in boys

   b. acne

   c. increased weight

   d. rheumatoid arthritis

3. Exercise during puberty is

   a. undesirable

   b. dangerous

   c. healthy and helpful

   d. too much of a strain on an already overtired body

4. Puberty may begin as early as:

   a. five years old in girls; seven years old in boys

   b. fifteen in girls; seventeen in boys

   c. eight in girls; ten in boys

   d. it begins at age twelve in both sexes

5. Voice changes in boys can be cured by:

   a. practising singing scales

   b. strength of will

   c. time

   d. taking hormonal shots

6. Puberty is:

   a. a time when there are serious medical problems

   b. a natural time of physical transformation from childhood to adulthood

   c. a time when many people find themselves to be abnormal

   d. a time when physical changes take place in exactly the same way at exactly the same time among all children.

7. Hormones are:

   a. natural body chemicals

   b. injections the doctor will give you

   c. small, time-releasing capsules you take orally

   d. brain waves

Activity 2

Visit the library—either the school or the local library—to find books on puberty and grooming. Bring in good magazine articles on these topics to share with students.

3   Doing

Evaluation

Activity 1

Check that students know the facts from Activity 1. Hold a discussion on the answers.

Activity 2

If possible, ask students share the information they found in the library. Try to encourage positive attitudes when they read this material.

Specific Resolutions

To have a positive, healthy attitude to the changes in the body and to respond with the appropriate body care.

Chapter 27
Stones on the Path

General Information

Topic

The changing moods of puberty and adolescence.

Content

- Moodiness.
- Coping with moodiness.
- Distinguishing natural moodiness from depression.

Objectives

Knowing
- Understanding why moods are part of puberty and adolescence.
- Appreciating that these moods need to kept under control.

Accepting
- Accepting that sometimes they will not feel well, but that it is the price of becoming an adult.
- To accept that they cannot allow their moods or feelings to inconvenience others.
- To see that they should show others the same understanding they expect to be given themselves.

Doing
- To show humour and courage in dealing with changing moods.

Areas of Human Development to be Emphasised

- Taking responsibility for one's own well-being.
- Taking responsibility for the well-being of others.

Class Plan

1   Knowing

Motivation

Ask students if they find themselves moody sometimes.

Story context:

Alice and Charlie are having a hard time coping with the moodiness of adolescence, but their friend Richard is having an especially hard time.

Introduction

Coping with normal adolescent moodiness is possible, but depression needs treatment.

Presentation

Key Ideas

- Some moodiness is normal, but they should try not to burden others too much.
- Moodiness can be transformed into something positive.
- There are significant differences between adolescent moodiness and real depression.

Topic Development

A   Moodiness

Alice is experiencing typical hormonally-induced moodiness. She is over-sensitive: *"I feel so sensitive— almost like I feel everything AMPLIFIED. I saw a sweet little dog on the street this morning—it made me cry because I thought it was lost. And I still felt upset even after its owner had appeared!"*

Her sensibilities are amplified. A stone on the path, a lost animal, seem to her like major tragedies. She cries easily and is easily upset by small obstacles (a stone on the path). This hypersensitivity, amplifying everything, being easily saddened, even feeling like an exposed raw nerve, are part of adolescence. Students may recognise some of this in themselves. Irritability, bad temper and sarcastic attitudes (often directed at parents and teachers) are part of this moodiness. Emphasise how adolescent moodiness can affect adults: they must try to monitor how these affect others.

B   Coping with moodiness

With humour and mutual support, Alice and Charlie are able to accept their moodiness and tease each other out of it: *"From then on, Alice and Charlie decided to have a signal they could give each other when one of them was feeling upset over nothing. "Hey, there's a hormone on the warpath—don't trip over it."*

Alice determines to try harder: *"Maybe I have been a bit over-sensitive—after all, I only tripped over and fell. Perhaps I should try not to let things get to me so much next time."*

Just recognising that one is in a hormone-induced mood can help counteract it: *"It's those hormones we were reading about the other day."*

Another helpful thing to do is to channel the energies away from oneself. Charlie and Alice gain energy and hope by deciding to help the kitten and the animal shelter.

As soon as Alice realised there was something she could do to help the kitten, her mood changed. She ran home and got a box, and then she and Charlie took the kitten to the local animal shelter.

Alice looked round the shelter. "It's sad, all those animals needing homes," she said seriously.

"Yes," said Charlie hesitantly, again waiting for tears.

"Well, maybe it's up to us younger people to do something—after all, we have more energy than older people! What about raising some money to help the shelter!"

"Or we could collect cans of pet food to donate," Charlie suggested.

"Or round up volunteers to help for free so there's more money for cages and stuff!" said Alice, breaking into a run.

Many, but not all, adults will understand adolescent moodiness: "Look at them!" he heard someone say as they ran past. "How wonderful to be young! No troubles! No worries! No problems!"

No problems? Well, some people have a short memory, thought Charlie.

C A Different Situation: Depression

A few teenagers, like Richard, may suffer constant, unwarranted feelings of sadness; this may lead to behavioural changes such as sleeping problems, waking up tired, continual lack of enthusiasm, concentration problems, and little capacity to enjoy life.

He kept saying things like, "What's the use?" whenever anyone suggested he did anything at all. He said that he was having trouble sleeping at night, then trouble getting up in the mornings. He even seemed to avoid his friends whenever he could.

To overcome this, it is important to acknowledge the reasons behind this sadness.

▸ If it is caused by concrete and identifiable situations, it is important to discover how sufferers interpret these situations. They probably do not look at these objectively, but from an acutely negative point of view ("It's terrible", "Nobody loves me", etc.) That way of thinking is what generates those sad feelings. We need to help students analyse their feelings objectively, and teach them to find new ways of solving problems that will cheer them up and help their future.

▸ However, when the source of sadness is internal, without showing an external trigger, this may be a case of depression. It is advisable to talk to the family and eventually get the school professionals involved, at least during the evaluation phase.

If the symptoms persist and we witness major behavioural change, it is necessary to talk with the family and urge them to seek treatment from a specialist. Ask students to read the next Inset in their Books (p.175):

Depression in Children and Teenagers:

There is Always Someone to Turn To

Childhood depression is much more common than most people realise. Often it is brought on by circumstances, and more occasionally there are clinical reasons which need to be professionally diagnosed.

There are many possible symptoms of depression. Some people become down, others hyperactive. Some can seem aggressive, others sad. Often, sufferers don't want to play with their friends any more, and they may start having difficulty in class. They tend to become irritable, to cry easily, and they may be less hungry and sleep badly.

> *If you think you or somebody else might be suffering from childhood depression, the important thing is to speak to a trusted adult as soon as you become concerned. It is usually best to talk to a member of your family or to a family friend. But if you would prefer to talk to somebody not so closely involved, you might want to choose a friendly teacher or the School Counsellor. Both will know whether a professional child therapist or psychiatrist should be brought in and they will be able to give appropriate help.*

2   Accepting

Guided Work

Activity 1

Ask students to do the exercises suggested in Activity 27A:

Activity 27

There is a 'flip side' to moodiness, like the other side of a coin. When you feel moody, think what good can come out of it.

Example 1: I feel sad when I see homeless people in the street.

List three things you can do to help the situation.

Example 2: I feel angry that my parents don't understand me.

Study communications techniques and then role-play different situations.

Example 3: I feel lonely

The best way to make friends is to be a friend. Instead of waiting for someone to call you, call your friends. Join a club at school. Write a letter to a relative who lives in another area, or make arrangements to give a party. Make a list of other ways to get in contact with people in a beneficial way.

Activity 2

Ask them to name three ways to help a homeless person.

Activity 3

Ask students in small groups to role-play some of the situations in Activity 27B (p.229). (This is to help them get over anger when their parents don't seem to understand them, and to gain communications skills to help their parents understand.)

Activity 27B:

> a. A boy wants to play football but his mother is worried that he'll get hurt.
>
> b. A girl wants her parents to get her a mobile.
>
> c. A boy wants to be allowed to play outside later than he is allowed to.
>
> d. A girl wants to be allowed to wear more makeup.
>
> e. A boy or girl wants more pocket money (or to receive pocket money).

Encourage them to see matters from their parents' point of view and argue with that in mind.

Activity 4

Give them class time to get in touch with a distant relative, friend, or classmate who has moved away.

3 Doing

Evaluation

Recognising moodiness for what it is goes a long way to help dealing with it. Encourage students to seek help early if they need it.

Students often come up with creative, funny, and wise solutions to difficulties. Observe their reasoning powers in trying to persuade their parents in the role-playing session. Give them the appreciation they deserve.

Specific Resolutions

To realise when they are being controlled by their moods, and to apply solutions: humour, sharing it with a friend, or turning it into a positive action to help someone or something else.

To be prepared to help someone who seems to be suffering from depression by consulting a responsible adult.

Chapter 28
Now!!

 General Information

Topic

Impatience and frustration.

Content

▶ Chafing under rules and regulations.
▶ Gaining perspective.
▶ Coping with impatience and frustration.

Objectives

Knowing
▶ Understanding impatience and its the characteristics.

Accepting
▶ Avoiding impatience and expressions of frustration.

Doing
▶ Trying to accept patiently adults' rules and regulations.

Areas of Human Development to be Emphasised

▶ Developing the virtue of patience.
▶ Seeing in perspective.

Class Plan

1   Knowing

Motivation

Ask students if they have ever felt there were too many rules in their lives. Ask if they have ever been grounded for breaking rules.

Story context:

Charlie has violated his curfew and must be patient throughout a week's grounding.

Introduction

Patience needs to be learned and practised, so as to cope with life's ups and downs.

Presentation

Key Ideas

▸   Rules and regulations are for protecting a child, not for hindrance.

▸   Patience is a learned virtue which takes practice.

▸   One's attitude can change everything.

Topic Development

A   Chafing under rules and regulations

A young person's growing wish for freedom and independence result in some impatience at the restrictions imposed by adults (see Chapter 1 on responsibility and freedom). Remind students that ignoring the rules and restrictions of healthy eating results in losing the freedom of mobility and good health. Traffic laws help smooth traffic flow and prevent jams, resulting in more freedom for everyone on the road. Fair and reasonable rules and restrictions lead to more freedom, not less.

Analyse with the class some of the restrictions Charlie's parents impose on him. Do students think the limits on Charlie's electronics time are for his own good? Numerous studies show that too much time spent on TV and video games increases aggression and decreases academic abilities. The rapid pace of children's programmes and games damages their concentration on reading, etc. Violent TV and video games increase conflict. They can also decrease sensitivity to violence—making violence seem a valid way to solve problems. Bandura's famous study[12] of children's levels of conflict after watching violent shows is one of many research studies showing a link between virtual and real life violence.

Statistics also show that children's health is adversely affected by excessive TV viewing. They exercise less and watch advertisements for junk food. They may also be subjected to cigarette and alcohol advertisements.

Above all this, the bombardment of sexual messages and unhealthy relationships can deeply affect their socialising capacity.

---

12.   Bandura, Albert. *Social Learning Theory.* Englewood Cliffs, N.J.: Prentice-Hall, 1977.

Charlie's parents care about him, which is why they try to limit his electronics time. Charlie's mother also explains why his parents take his curfew seriously: *"You know it's for your own safety. If you don't come home at the agreed time, we don't know what's happened to you."* Although he is given freedom to be out unsupervised with his friends for certain periods of time, his parents, to ensure his safety and to prevent their worrying about him, insist that he report in at certain times.

B Coping with impatience and frustration

Charlie learns about coping with impatience and frustration from watching Silver Lining, the homeless cat he cares for. Like Charlie, the kitten doesn't want to be confined: *It got out of the box straight away. Charlie watched it fall awkwardly to the floor. Then it ran round all the edges of the room. Charlie began to feel sorry for it. Suddenly a thought occurred to Charlie. He's like me—he told himself—he doesn't want to be confined.* But the kitten quickly adapts, contenting himself with bathing, eating, napping, and playing with the children. Because of the kitten, the weekend flew by.

Charlie is advised both by his mother and Alice to be patient, view the situation positively, and concentrate on interests at home. Taking it step by step, Charlie survives, planning his free time around school, work, and at-home recreation. His relatives help him—his brother challenges him to several chess games, and Alice provides the kitten: the 'silver lining'—he wouldn't have been able to take care of him if he hadn't been grounded.

C Gaining perspective

Transitory problems may appear much more long-lasting and major than they really are, especially to the adolescent. Several ways to change our perspective are outlined in the Guided Work section. One important means is to reinterpret people's actions in a charitable way. This change often happens naturally: the late friend who has left us waiting outside the cinema defuses our impatience and anger in mentioning that his ill mother called just as he was leaving.

New York bus drivers—people with very stressful jobs—are trained to reinterpret the maddening behaviour of passengers. The drivers are shown a film of people not cooperating with the bus drivers—then shown that the person is ill, on medication, or in pain. A person may seem drunk but actually is suffering from cerebral palsy; a person having a mild epileptic fit may appear to be ignoring the bus driver's directions. A person asking repeatedly where her street is may be suffering from severe anxiety and unable to help herself. Patient people interpret other people's actions charitably: when cut off in traffic, they assume that the offender has to get to a hospital emergency or a house on fire.[13]

While not all actions can be interpreted charitably—sometimes people do behave wrongly, cruelly, unjustly—it is sensible to give the benefit of the doubt, since one rarely knows all the facts. At the least, it leads to greater calm and content!

2 Accepting

Guided Work

Activity 1

Ask students to read Activity 28A in their Books (p.230), which reinforces some ways to build patience outlined in the story—and to write or discuss conclusions and purposes:

---

13.   *See further:* Tavris, Carol. *Anger: the Misunderstood Emotion.* Tappan, NJ: Touchstone, 1989. ISBN 0671675230

Activity 28 A

Read the following and see how these relate to things that you may have felt.

Taking things step by step helps build patience. Believing that 'every cloud has a silver lining' is a good way to be patient with difficult situations.

Another way to be patient with your situation is to sympathise with someone who is less fortunate than you are. Charlie had a homeless cat who was within a hair's breadth of death, who couldn't be allowed to go out either.

Charlie could have compared himself with Anne Frank, the 12-year-old author of a diary that was found after her death. Anne's family was in hiding from the Nazis for over a year. They had to be quiet all day long in a confined place and they lived in fear of discovery. Anne contented herself with writing in her diary, and her diary has been an inspiration to countless people ever since.

Activity 2

Ask students to re-read the Taoist story of the lost horse in Activity 21, p.226. Viewing situations so philosophically builds patience in adversity. Ask students in groups to discuss the story and the consequences in it with regard to patience.

Activity 3

Ask students to reinterpret the situations in Activity 28C (p.232) charitably and with patience:

Activity 28 C

1. Someone is in front of your locker and you want them to get out of the way. Instead of saying, "Move!" you tell yourself:

....

....

2. A teacher seems to be forgetting a lot lately and losing things. Instead of blaming and accusing him or her of being stupid, you think:

....

....

3. Your Mum says she can't help you with your homework. Instead of thinking she's being mean, you think:

....

....

4. Your dad tells you to turn the volume down on the TV. Instead of thinking he's an old fogey, you think

....

....

3   Doing

End by highlighting the importance of viewing a situation from a humorous or more charitable perspective, always recognising its transitory nature so as to have patience.

Activity 1

Ask students to share ideas on all the possible conclusions. Emphasise strategies to develop patience.

Activity 2

As a class activity, analyse the consequences that each group came up with. Help students to shift their focus to see things more clearly and learn patience.

Activity 3

In class, share ideas for correctly solving each situation. Point out the contrast between correct and incorrect ways.

Specific Resolution

To tackle with humour, perspective, and optimism all situations which produce frustration and impatience.

Chapter 29
Learning Your Limits—Soothing Irritability

General Information

Topic

Irritability.

Content

▶ Irritability in adolescence.

▶ Ways to handle irritability, including prevention.

Objectives

Knowing

▶ Irritability is a normal characteristic of adolescence, but we must learn to regulate it.

Accepting

▶ Being patient and aware of our own irritability.

Doing

▶ Learning to channel irritable feelings.

▶ Apologising when these get out of hand.

▶ Acquiring basic skills to control irritability.

▶ Avoiding projecting our irritability onto others.

Areas of Human Development to be Emphasised

▶ Healthy habits.

▶ Self-regulation.

Class Plan

1   Knowing

Motivation

Ask students what things irritate them most. What really infuriates them? Then tell them this chapter is about dealing with irritability.

Story context:

Charlie is irritated by his mother, his cousin, and the physical after-effects of eating too much chocolate.

Introduction

Natural adolescent irritability is compounded by unwise choices in diet, sleep habits, over-stimulation, etc.

Presentation

Key Ideas

▸ Stress and irritability result from the conflict between independence and the continuing need for parental care and guidance.

▸ Adolescents tend to let themselves be overstimulated.

▸ Moderation and self-care are needed to prevent and soothe irritability.

Topic Development

A   Irritability in adolescence

A sure way to irritate adolescents is to treat them like children! This story shows some of the tension between the need at times for parental care and the desire at others to break away from this care. The story opens with Charlie showing this irritation:

"Mum!" said Charlie peevishly. "Stop kissing me all the time!"

Dad looked up from the paper. "He's not a baby," he said.

*"Well, he'll always be **my** baby," said Mum with a smile.*

Here we go, thought Charlie—they're off on their usual dialogue, Mum saying she's just being a mother and Dad saying that she has to let me grow up.

Yet when Charlie feels unwell, he appreciates his mother's care. When his father accuses her of "babying" him again, he shouts in annoyance, *"Maybe I need a little extra attention sometimes! I don't feel well!"* But he realises that he often welcomes his dad's view that she should give him more independence, so he apologises reluctantly.

At the end of the story a comic parallel is drawn with the cat, who also does not want to be smothered with affection, when Emily keeps him in her bed all night:

But it soon became clear that, though Charlie might not have been irritable about it, Silver was. He seemed to have had enough kissing and cuddling to last a lifetime! He shot out of Emily's bed, hissing and spitting at anyone he passed, and went off to clean himself in peace.

"He's feeling irritable," Mum observed.

"Don't worry, Silver," said Charlie soothingly. "I know just how you feel!"

Adolescents have to differentiate themselves from their parents and establish a new identity. This strains the old alliance with parents and family of origin as the new 'person' tries to grow. Yet the old ties are still very strong. Both yearnings—to be independent while still belonging to the family—are a huge hurdle for adolescents. They additionally have to cope with raging hormones and newly complex relationships with the opposite sex, so their irritability is not surprising.

Since some irritability is natural, adolescents need coping strategies. One method is to give irritability its name. Charlie's mother helps him identify his state of mind, explaining why irritability is common at his age. Alice also rebukes him for his bad mood. Just naming a state of mind sometimes eases it (the Activity section gives more detail).

Charlie has also made some unwise health choices in the story which are adding to his irritability: *Last night Dad had agreed that he and Louis could stay up and watch an action film, even though Mum wasn't happy about it because it was a Thursday. Then he had hardly slept because some of the images in the film kept going through his   head. Consequently, he had found it almost impossible to get up this morning, and now he had to go to school.*

Charlie, hoping to wake himself up, compounds his state of physical and mental exhaustion by consuming not nutritious food but sugary chocolate bars for lunch. *He found his head buzzing for a while, and then he felt sick.*

Remind students that too much of a good thing causes an ill effect. Even happy events—like a new house, a new baby in the family, a gift of money—can cause irritability and stress. Students should constantly look out for irritability.

Charlie is also over-stimulated by the idea of going to a film that night with Alice and Marianne. In consequence he gets a stomach-ache and headache. His mother has him drink some soup, rest, and forego the film. She tells him *just to relax. She said even social events could be stressful. She said that a certain amount of irritability was natural in a boy of Charlie's age and that he had to try to soothe himself when he felt irritated, and not overdo things. She was certain he needed more sleep—the hormones secrete at night, so he needed to give them a chance to do their work of turning him into a man. She said Charlie needed a better diet, too, if he wasn't going to be super-irritable.*

Charlie actually feels relief at this. After nourishment and a peaceful, good night's sleep among his family, Charlie awakens with his irritability gone.

Charlie wasn't imagining he would enjoy going to bed at eight o'clock, while everybody else was still up. But, to his surprise, he did. Mum tucked him in and drew the curtains, just as she had done when he was little. And tomorrow was Saturday, so he could sleep late. The soup was settling his stomach, and, as his head relaxed, he fell into a deep, soothing sleep.

Charlie woke up next morning feeling like a new person.

"How's the crank?" asked Louis at breakfast.

"Cranky no more," replied Charlie serenely.

2   Accepting

Guided Work

Activity 1

Ask students to look at Activity 29A in their Books (p.233) and to justify their choice.

Activity 29 A

> You have a ton of homework, your Mum has chores lined up for you, and your room is such a mess, you can't find the things you need. You feel pressured and want to yell at the world. Choose an effective method of dealing with all this:
>
> 1.   Decide to do some work, then reward yourself, more work, then reward yourself. Start small and build up, resting in between.
>
> 2.   Go out and tell your mother angrily that she should help you clean up your room, help you do your homework, and that she should do the chores herself to take pressure off you.
>
> 3.   Watch a really exciting, stimulating movie (preferably an action film) to take your mind off things.

Activity 2

Explain briefly the model of Steven Stosny (below)[14]. Then analyse together the example of irritability expressed there.

Ask students to think about other irritating scenarios, based on their own major causes of anger that they named at the beginning of class. Ask them to counteract them with the 3 steps below.

Psychologist Steven Stosny gives a 3-Step model for converting negative feelings (like irritability) into interest and enjoyment.

▶   **Step 1:** Validate the feeling. (Identify and name it, e.g. "I feel irritable.")

▶   **Step 2:** Experience it momentarily.

▶   **Step 3:** Change it into interest or enjoyment by

    a.   telling yourself it is OK to experience interest and enjoyment

    b.   rewarding yourself for accomplishing interest and enjoyment.

Guide students through this 'irritable' example:

Scenario: I'm irritated that my brother is watching his favourite TV show when I want to watch something else.

▶   **Step 1:** I am irritable.

▶   **Step 2:** I really want that TV for myself but I can't get it and that's a stupid show he likes, anyway.

▶   **Step 3:**

    a.   The show is only a half hour long. Why don't I go and read the magazine

       I have in my room. I've been looking forward to reading it.

---

14.   Op. cit., see footnote on p. 88.

b. I'm glad I can do something so interesting. My favourite show is on after my brother's. That will be good too. I'm glad I have more than one interest.

3 Doing

Evaluation

Activity 1

Ask students to choose the most effective method and discuss it with the class. Comment too on the possible results when choosing other methods. Try to emphasise the harm in depending on others and also in taking the easy way out. Emphasise the advantages of facing the situation and resolving it little by little.

Activity 2

Once students have used the Stosny Model for a particular case, reinforce its use by carefully selecting a student who can tell the rest of the class how to use the model. If you wish, the students may work in groups and apply the Model to a fictitious situation.

Emphasise how common irritability is at their age; urge them to cope with it by using the methods discussed in this lesson.

Specific Resolutions

To identify irritability as it is happening.

To identify possible physical causes of irritability which can be remedied.

To channel irritability into interest and enjoyment.

Chapter 30
Communication

General Information

Topic

Communication and its advantages.

Content

▶ Communication as the basis of family life.
▶ Communications techniques: the Mirror.
▶ Communication and love.

Objectives

Knowing
▶ Understanding the advantages and techniques of good communication.

Accepting
▶ Cultivating good communication to resolve family conflict.
▶ Appreciating good communication within the family.

Doing
▶ To try to build bridges when necessary, to encourage communication within the family.

Areas of Human Development to be Emphasised

▶ Assertiveness.
▶ Self-control.

Class Plan

1   Knowing

Motivation

Ask students how they act when they feel angry. How do they deal with people who make them angry? Does this usually help or hurt the situation? The relationship?

Story context

Charlie applies communication techniques learnt at school to some family annoyances.

Introduction

Charlie learns various aspects of communication in anger and in love.

Presentation

Key Ideas

▶   Communication is important.

▶   Techniques can help resolve conflict situations.

▶   The most important things to communicate are feelings.

Topic Development

A   Communication as the basis of family life

Remind students that they are always communicating something. Even refusing to speak to someone communicates anger or rejection or pain.

Mention 'body language'—it shows a lot about us and our feelings. Shifty eyes can worry people by suggesting dishonesty (but the person may just be shy). A limp handshake gives an impression of weakness and disturbs the other person. Arms crossed over the chest show the wish to protect oneself and be closed off. Toes turned inward denote insecurity.

Other ways of non-verbal communication include tone of voice, facial expression, etc.

Because family members are with us so often and at such close quarters, smooth communication in this setting is particularly important. Yet the family is where most people feel they can 'let down their hair' and where they think they don't need to adhere to the usual norms of polite behaviour, but can just 'be themselves'. Actually, they should be even more polite and kind in the intimate setting of family life.

Humans yearn for intimacy, wanting to be very close to at least a few others. Being intimate with others makes us feel emotionally safe with them—that shared activity is made better because we did it together. Something as simple as washing up or buying groceries becomes enjoyable because of intimacy with another in the shared activity.

Sometimes, however, we will inevitably be angry, hurt, annoyed, in a bad or negative mood. Sometimes the cause is outside the family. If we frequently communicate bad feelings in a negative, harsh way, eventually intimacy becomes impaired.

B   Communication Techniques: The Mirror

Communication techniques can help with this. The best-known one is the 'mirror technique'—also called the 'reflective listening technique' or 'structured dialogue'. Charlie has Louis and Giselle practise it.

This technique consists in sending 'I' messages (how I respond or react when you…) rather than 'you' messages ("You really make me mad when you…"), which are more accusatory. A person who has agreed to the mirror technique, as Louis did, has to reflect back accurately to the first person what that person said to ensure it has been understood. The first person, after confirming that the message has been understood, is prompted to reveal any other feelings by the partner's asking, "Is there more?"

When Louis and Giselle use this technique Giselle discovers that Louis's annoying habit is not because he doesn't care—he simply forgets. Also, he thinks she's a wonderful sister whom he would choose above all others.

As Charlie found with his dad, a short cooling off period may be needed before trying to communicate in a volatile situation. Charlie's dad does not know the mirror technique, but Charlie's careful approach of waiting until his father is relaxed and then sending 'I' messages communicates to him Charlie's feelings, and their quarrel is settled.

C   Communication and love

Experts say that only 7% of communication is verbal. Body language and attitude convey the rest. A kindly, loving, sincere underlying motive that wants to make amends will be communicated 'between the lines'. A sneaky, self-serving attitude of wanting to ingratiate oneself for selfish purposes, or any insincerity, will also be evident.

If people love each other, their communication will usually reflect this. Communication techniques cannot replace love and good intentions—as Charlie finds with his father:

"I'm sorry I seem gruff sometimes, and react too quickly," Dad said. "Mum tells me off about it. But if I worry about you, even unnecessarily, it's because I would blame myself if anything bad happened to any of you."

Dad turned on the TV again, and they watched quietly for a few minutes. Really, his dad could be cringe-makingly soft sometimes, Charlie reflected. And he could get cross. But now at least he understood why Dad made rules—he only did it because he cared for him.

At the same time, Charlie's use of communication techniques has helped build this time of sharing and helped them resolve a conflict.

2   Accepting

Guided Work

Activity 1

Ask students to look at Activity 30A in their books (p.233), to analyse the case and respond briefly.

Activity 30 A

> Your dad is yelling at you for starting the car with his keys while you were waiting for him. What might your dad really be feeling? Is he really worried about your safety?
>
> What kind of things might he be imagining might happen?

Activity 2

Ask students, in groups, to look at Activity 30B in their Books (p.233), to analyse the scenario and choose the best answer. They should be able to justify their choice to the rest of the class.

Activity 30 B

> Your Mum comes into your room. She says, "I'm sorry I accused you of taking money out of my purse without asking. I forgot that I said you could take some lunch money for school. I don't want you to get in the habit of going in my purse, but I shouldn't have been cross with you." Which of these are good responses:
>
> a. "That's okay, Mum. I know you want to teach me good standards."
>
> b. "Well, I'm sick and tired of you yelling when you don't know what's what!"
>
> c. "That's OK, Mum. Only I wish you'd give me a little more time to explain before you yell at me."
>
> d. "Take your money then—you care more about money than you do about me!"

Activity 3

Ask for student volunteers to practise the mirror technique in front of the class—as many as want to. Perhaps two students have had a recent, not-too-serious conflict they would be willing to act out. Ask them first to read the rules in Activity 30C (p.234).

Activity 30 C

> Rules for the mirror technique:
>
> a. The one who feels strongest about the conflict starts.
>
> b. He or she sends 'I' messages about how he or she was affected emotionally (keeping statements short!)
>
> c. The other person reflects back what the first person has said and must receive confirmation from the first person that he or she reflected it back accurately. Then he or she prompts, "Is there more?"
>
> d. When the first person has fully expressed his or her feelings, it is the other's turn.

Many people are surprised at what this technique brings out. Often, they find that the other party's motives were quite different from what they thought they were. Often, sympathy and good will are created or regained.

3   Doing

Evaluation

Activity 1

In class ask students to analyse the most frequent answers to the questions. It's important that they 'stand in their parents shoes' to be as objective as they can. Emphasise that our attitude is the main issue in communication. No techniques can replace respect for the other person. However, communication techniques provide a safe basis for tackling tough issues, increasing the possibility of trust and intimacy.

Activity 2

In class, ask groups to justify their answers to their classmates. Clearly a. is the best answer, but c. is more realistic. Ask students to consider answers a.–d. and discuss what the mother might have said next.

Activity 3

While they practise the mirror technique, try to help the reluctant students understand the importance of rules for good communication.

Specific Resolution

During this week, when conflicts arise, to try the mirror technique or do as Charlie does: let things calm down a bit and try sending 'I' messages.

Abilities:
* To understand that caring for health is increasingly the student's own responsibility and that there will be peer pressure to behave negatively.
* To realise that health includes mental and spiritual as well as physical health.
* To know the dangers of pornography and masturbation.
* To know the importance of exercise, sleep and diet.
Number of Chapters: 5 (31 to 34).

Chapter 31
'Blondie'

General Information

Topic

Pornography.

Content

▶ Pornography is addictive.
▶ The effects of consumption of pornography:
a. on the individual
b. on society.
▶ The pornography industry.
▶ Consumption of pornography shows emotional immaturity and arrested. development of personality.

Objectives

Knowing
▶ Understanding the effects of pornography.

Accepting
▶ To avoid pornography as it is self-destructive behaviour.
▶ To value modesty.

Doing
▶ To know how to avoid or refuse pornography.

Areas of Human Development to be Emphasised

▶ Respect for self and others.

▶ Self-control.

▶ Social awareness.

Class Plan

1   Knowing

Motivation

Explain to students that if they have not already been exposed to pornography, they almost certainly will be, even by accident (through internet pop-ups, which the user had not intended to access).

Story context:

Charlie is offered some pornography. Even a quick look affects him; he wonders about the right and wrong of it and submits the question to Mr Radigan, the health officer, who then addresses the issue in class.

Introduction

The damage pornography does to the individual and society is explored in detail.

Presentation

Key Ideas

▶ Pornography is addictive by nature.

▶ Pornography encourages disrespect and crime.

▶ Pornography is harmful to individuals and society.

▶ Pornography retards maturity.

Topic Development

A   Pornography is addictive

Pornography acts like addictive drugs: it is extremely stimulating at first, but then a person needs increasingly more to feel the same initial stimulation—or else a variety that can very quickly turn into increasingly twisted and violent images.

As Mr Radigan says, *"It is addictive. It works just like a drug—you have to have more to get the same rush you got the first time. In fact, that's a classic feature of addiction."* He goes on to say of its addictive qualities: *"Use of pornography may start casually. …But soon it will start to dominate your thoughts. Eventually, you may even begin to arrange your life around it. It is possible to start preferring it to the company of real people, in which case your relationships suffer. With some people it escalates and they need more, or more twisted, even violent, kinds to get stimulated. They get less and less sensitive to it and to the standards of the community."*

B   Effects of pornography

On the individual

Pornography substitutes for real, true and satisfying relationships because it is more readily found. Charlie realised that he could go to the alley anytime and see any amount of girls *he wanted. It would be almost like having a date.*

However, Charlie wonders if it is wrong, and asks Ron's older brother, Jason, for advice. Jason says "*It's natural*" *and* "*Nobody gets hurt.*" Charlie later learns that Jason is causing his parents so much trouble that his own parents wonder if it is safe to let Charlie keep company with him. Clearly, he is not a good source of advice.

Further effects on the individual are that the user begins to see women *"through the lens of pornography. Pornography shows women as sexual objects to be sniggered and salivated over-used and discarded. ...It encourages disrespect for, and mistreatment of, women—your mothers, your sisters, your classmates, your friends. The person using pornography just sees them as sexual targets for his fantasies. Do you like the idea of some man thinking those kinds of thoughts about the women you know and love? That's the sort of thinking pornography encourages."*

Most people do not want their relatives—sisters and mothers—to be seen through the lens of pornography, but do not realise how it distorts the user's view of women.

The individual is also being exploited. *"Pornography uses your natural appreciation for the beauty of females (and external beauty is just part of a girl's beauty, of course). Your sexual desire—a wonderful gift given to you for the sake of love and having children—is being used and twisted by people who only care about money."*

Also, pornography users damage their own sex life and chances of satisfaction: *"In the end, pornography spoils sexual activity between husband and wife. Because it focuses only on the body, it can never bring total satisfaction, because sexuality involves the mind and heart too. And then, because the pictures are cut and airbrushed to make the girls look perfect, they set up a comparison that a real woman can't live up to. Even worse, it may not be just the pictures that are altered, but the girls themselves—through surgery."*

On society

Because pornography treats women as mere objects, causing distortions of women's true nature in the minds of men, it is strongly linked to crime:

"A presidential report found a link between the murder of women and the use of pornography. [15] *And serial killers have said that pornography drove them to do what they did.* [16] *In fact, many studies show a link between looking at pornography and committing sexual offences."* [17]

He also notes that some of the 'stars' of pornography are forced to pose like that. *"Many of those people in pictures and in movies do it because they are drug addicts or have run away and they are desperate."*

Charlie thinks of this when he remembers Blondie: *Suddenly 'Blondie' didn't seem so attractive to Charlie. Was she a drug addict? Suppose she was being forced to pose like that? Maybe she had AIDS?*

Mr Radigan hates telling students about these shocking and horrible things, but it is important for them to know the destructive and dangerous reality of pornography.

---

15.   Attorney General Meese's Commission's Presidential Report on Pornography, 1988.

16.   Bender, David, ed. *Is Pornography Harmful?* San Diego, CA: Greenhaven Press, 1989. p.142.

17.   Attison, Julie A. and Wrightsman, Laurence S. *Rape: the Misunderstood Crime.* Newbury Park: Sage, 1993. pp. 37-44.

C   The pornographic industry

Pornography is a frighteningly huge industry, netting vast annual sums for its producers—sometimes more than all other forms of entertainment combined. It is like a 'shadow industry'—organised crime, which deals in drugs and prostitution as well.

Pornography is like a huge cancer on society, and flourishes on consumption. Without a demand for it, there would be no supply, and the perpetrators would be bankrupt. Each individual decision to avoid contact with pornography means less demand. Urge your students not to feed this industry by consuming pornography in any way, whatever.

D   Consuming pornography shows arrested development and emotional immaturity

As Mr Radigan says, not all pornography users become rapists, killers, or child molesters. However, pornography keeps the user at an arrested level of development. We develop and grow through relationships with real people, not through fantasies and pictures. Sometimes, as Mr Radigan says, a man is simply not mature enough to deal with a real woman. He can only deal with images. Images, however, do not talk, or have an opinion, or disagree, or need love or sacrifice from the man, or require him to grow as a person. He can pretend that the image of the woman loves him instead of having to win a real woman's love, which takes effort. As Mr Radigan notes, *"So that man will just carry on living in a fantasy-land and never learn how to love unselfishly."*

Reality can be difficult, but it also fulfils our deepest longings. It can never be replaced by a fantasy.

2   Accepting

Guided Work

Activity 1

Imagery is powerful. Ask students if any of them has retained persistent memories of a film. Films with violent or emotionally evocative images can affect us long afterwards.

Activity 2

Advertisers know the power of images. They pay vast sums to get the image of their product into people's minds.

Suggest students do a research project on the influence of advertising images on behaviour. Ask small groups to conduct a brief research on the topic.

Activity 3

To help students understand the power of visual imagery, experiment with a bottle of clear soda. Put different coloured food dyes in small samples of the soda, e.g. brown, orange or yellow to resemble popular fizzy drinks. Ask students to sip each one and compare the tastes. Maybe a few will say they all taste the same, but many or most will think there is a difference because of the appearance. Explain that the drinks were all the same, just different in colour. Appearances can be deceiving.

Activity 4

Ask students to list the ways that pornography can be linked to crime. Then ask them how pornography can keep a person in a state of emotional immaturity and arrested personal development.

3   Doing

Evaluation

Activity 1

Discuss with the students the impact of the images. Suggest why it is best to avoid certain images and how difficult it can be, once in, to get such pictures out of the mind. Be sure that the students understand what you are getting at.

Activity 2

During a future class, you may want to analyse the results of the investigation to show how powerful advertisements can be.

Activity 3

Hold a class discussion to ensure that students have a good understanding about the criminal nature of pornography as well as the effects it has on personality development.

The conclusion should be: it's a crime that leads us into acting like naughty children instead of as mature adults.

Specific Resolution

To reject the use of all forms of pornography at all times.

Chapter 32
Solitary 'Pleasures'

General Information

Topic

Masturbation.

Content

▶ What is masturbation?

▶ Is it healthy: a) mentally; b) physically?

▶ Pleasure versus happiness.

▶ Combating masturbation.

▶ A matter of maturity.

Objectives

Knowing

▶ The difference between pleasure and happiness.

▶ Masturbation is seeking pleasure outside the natural context.

▶ Understanding the workings of the male body.

Accepting

▶ Rejecting masturbation as self-abuse.

▶ Cultivating strength and self-control to avoid the habit of masturbation.

Doing

▶ Respecting the body and sexuality so as to avoid self-abuse.

Areas of Human Development to be Emphasised

▶ Self-control.

▶ Preparation for intimacy as opposed to isolation.

Class Plan

1   Knowing

Motivation

Acknowledge that discussing this topic is embarrassing. Assure students that no personal questions will be asked of them. Mention that, like pornography, masturbation is primarily, although not solely, a male problem.

Story context:

Mr Radigan continues his health and hygiene classes, and focuses on masturbation.

Introduction

Masturbation is not healthy for the mind or the body.

Presentation

Key Ideas

▸   Some people erroneously believe that masturbation is harmless—even healthy.

▸   The relational effects are the most serious, but there can also be physical effects.

Topic Development

A   What is masturbation?

Start with Mr Radigan's definition: *The primary organs used in sexual intimacy are the genital organs. We all know how sensitive they are—get kicked in the wrong place and you really know about it! But rub or stroke the genital organs and the sensation is altogether different: it gives a sense of pleasure, the pleasure which is intended for intercourse. This is called masturbation.*

B   Is it healthy: a) mentally; b) physically?

Some people, including some medical experts, believe that masturbation, far from being harmful, is actually healthy. This stance is questionable on the physical level, and contradicts the evidence on the psychological level since everybody agrees that it can isolate a person from others socially.

As to the physical effects of masturbation, a regular habit becomes rough on the penis. The blood vessels of the male pelvic region become gorged and congested with blood. These vessels are very long and irregular, and if they become congested, they can form little pockets (the technical term is micro-diverticuli) that can easily harbour bacteria. Infections in this area of the body are hard to reach with antibiotics because it is so well-protected by nature. So these infections can go on for a long time, and they can cause permanent damage—even sterility. Male sterility is on the rise at present, and looser attitudes towards masturbation could be a contributing factor.[18] I should say that these risks are small and they are not going to come about from occasional lapses. But they are another reason why the habit is worth avoiding.

As Mr Radigan points out in answer to Alan's question about 'wet dreams': *they happen in your sleep— they're beyond your power to control. The formal name for them is 'nocturnal emissions'. It's when your body*

---

18.   Isidori, Aldo. *Etica della Andrologia* [= *Ethics of Andrology*]. Palermo: G.Russo, 2003. (*The author is Professor of Andrology at La Sapienza University*).

See also Nieschlag, E. and Behre, W. *Andrology: Male Reproductive Health and Dysfunction.* Berlin: Springer, 2001.

158

releases semen in the night. That's your body's natural way of releasing itself—you can't stop it or make it happen. You just have to trust your body to take care of releasing itself in that way."

Alan mentions that masturbation can have the healthy effect of releasing stress. However, Mr Radigan says, "There are better ways to reduce stress."

Emotionally, masturbation requires fantasy—a type of unhealthy mental pornography.

Eric Erickson calls the phase of psycho-sexual development that follows adolescence 'intimacy versus isolation'. Without success in this phase, life is incomplete. It depends upon success in earlier phases. Masturbation is an isolated affair. When Alan mentions that masturbation can help people learn what gives them pleasure, Mr Radigan replies:

"It teaches us about pleasuring ourselves, not someone else. It's self-centred. Being with another person is very different. Masturbation means you've learned a lot of sexual responses that are not suitable with another person. It takse away the 'us,' or the mutual pleasure dance of sexual response."

Masturbation is like playing solitaire and then hoping to be good at games like bridge that require a partner. It teaches nothing about rewarding relationships that are integral to social and sexual life, and which must be built with effort, virtue, and skill.

C Pleasure versus happiness

Life's pleasures need a right context. The examples of 'freedom' in Chapter 1 could be reviewed. Freedom is always linked to responsibility. If we eat only on impulse, ignoring the body's need for proper nutrition, we will become unhealthy and fat, and lose out accordingly. Any pleasure must be taken with a responsible attitude;,if indulged in the wrong way or circumstances, at the wrong time, or with the wrong person, so-called 'pleasures' lead to unhappiness.

Sexual pleasure is meant to be shared between husband and wife. Mr Radigan says of it, *"It nurtures closeness and intimacy. The endorphins and oxytocins which are released in sexual activity are intended to make us feel bonded to one another and fulfilled. The problem with masturbation is that these hormones are released only in relationship to ourselves, and the fulfilment is a cheat.*

Masturbation also diminishes us as people because it ignores the respect due to the gift of procreation. To take part in giving life to another human being is an awesome responsibility and should be treated accordingly. Mr Radigan says: *"There is another reason why masturbation isn't good for us, and that is that it reduces the respect we should have for the gift of fatherhood. The ability to give life is very precious. It's bigger than us, something which goes beyond us, something which is touched by mystery."*

Emphasise that the purpose of sex is not physical pleasure—this occurs incidentally. The whole person, mind, heart, body and soul, is involved. It should be a bonding act of intimacy within the context of total commitment. Then it leads to happiness with another person, not just the empty pleasure of yielding to uncontrolled sexual impulses.

D Combating masturbation

Mr Radigan gives some practical tips for avoiding masturbation, centring round right attitudes to those of the opposite sex—they are precious people, not objects for pleasure. *"Avoid situations that lead to thinking about sex. We've already spoken about pornography. But there are other things. For example, don't listen to sexy songs or talk about sex. Avoid dirty jokes—either telling them or listening to them."* He advises against spending a lot of time in bed, daydreaming or listening to music. He suggests instead that students release their energy by playing sports, going for walks, running, and getting going physically. That way they will also feel much better.

E   **A matter of maturity**

Like the use of pornography, masturbation retards the maturing process because it isolates one from healthy relationships, which stimulate growth. Often, people use it to escape their problems.

Charlie sees this point well demonstrated after Mr Radigan's talk: *After class, Charlie was surprised how much most of the boys seemed to just take Mr Radigan's talk in their stride. It was quite a contrast to last week, he thought, when there had been a lot of sniggering after the pornography session. Oh well, they were all growing up, he supposed. That's the funny thing about becoming a man, he mused. The very things you think make you grown up and manly—like playing around with your sexuality—are the very things that make you remain a boy.*

2   Accepting

Guided Work

Emphasise that we do not judge or condemn others. Students need this perspective to help them choose options that will contribute to a healthy and happy life.

Activity 1

Ask students to think about situations in which people act in a self-centred way, and the ill effects this has on others and society. Newspapers may be helpful in this. The story of a crime, for instance, might show the criminal disregarding other people's rights or property for his own enrichment.

Encourage students to analyse the self-centred elements in these situations. Is it good for people to do things that encourage self-centredness?

Activity 2

Ask students to talk about situations (it could be from their own lives) when someone acted altruistically (for the benefit of others). What benefits came from acting this way?

Again, newspaper stories about altruism, a Good Samaritan, benevolent groups, etc, could be used to show how acting for others benefits society.

Activity 3

Ask students, in groups, to answer the questions in Activity 32 in their Books (p.235).

Activity 32

> We've spoken before in this book about there being no freedom without responsibility.
>
> 1.   How do 'free' attitudes about sexual matters take away from our freedom and the freedom of others?
>
> 2.   What is the difference between 'pleasure' and 'happiness'? Which one is temporary, which is lasting? Name some things in life that can bring us pleasure but leave us unhappy in the end.
>
> 3.   Name some things that are pleasant in life, but lead to unhappiness in the end.

3 Doing

Evaluation

Activity 1

In class, moderate a debate between several students or between the whole class on the situations they have looked at.

Explain that criminals start with small selfish acts and progress to serious crime.

Activity 2

List positive examples, contrasting them with the results from Activity 1. It is better if the results of both exercises provide a positive vision.

Activity 3

In class, ask each group to find common answers to the 3 questions.

Hold a debate, allowing all students to speak. Ensure that students understand that sexual pleasure now might hurt their chances for future happiness; happiness, on the other hand, includes pleasure, which is part, for instance, of a happy marriage.

Specific Resolution

From the perspective of physical and mental health, to make the best possible choices—not to masturbate.

Chapter 33
Rebel with a Cause

General Information

Topic

The importance of physical activity to maintain health of body and mind.

Content

▶ How much physical activity do 11-12-year-olds need?
▶ What kinds of foods do they need?
▶ What are the benefits of healthy activities and snacks?

Objectives

Knowing
▶ Understanding the importance and benefits of physical activity.
▶ Understanding the benefits of sensible eating.

Accepting
▶ Cultivating physical activity to channel the energies of the human body.
▶ Appreciating sensible eating.

Doing
▶ Doing sufficient physical activities of the right sort.
▶ Using healthy moderation in eating.

Areas of Human Development to be Emphasised

▶ Responsibility.
▶ Self-respect.

Class Plan

1   Knowing

Motivation

Ask students how many of them enjoy sports, how many engage in other physical activities, and whether they enjoy school breaks and opportunities for physical activity.

Story context:

Alan asks Alice's help to persuade the Head to make some healthy changes at school.

Introduction

Physical activities and healthy eating benefit us in many ways, including academically.

Presentation

Key Ideas

▶   Children need a lot of physical activity.

▶   Children need healthy foods.

Topic Development

A   How much physical activity do 11-12-year-olds need?

In this unexpected collaboration between Alan and Alice, a student delegation approaches Mr Murphy, the Headteacher, to ask for an afternoon break between lunch and the end of the school day—a period of two and a half hours. Alan has done some research and found that the National Association for Health and Fitness recommends that no child go more than two hours without physical activity. The same association is raising its activity guidelines for children to several hours a day. Alice says: *"They recommend physical activity before school, during at least two breaks and during PE."*

B   What kinds of foods do a 11-12-year-olds need?

Alice refers to research showing that *"Young people our age need healthy snacks. We need nutrient-dense foods high in complex carbohydrates, moderate in protein, salt, and sugar, and low in fat and cholesterol. …Our snack machines have fizzy drinks, sweets and chocolate—all things we should eat moderately or not at all. So we would like to ask that the snack and drink machines sell juices and healthier, more nutritious snacks. We think that would improve our concentration too."*

Because puberty starts at around this age, boys and girls need protein: meat, poultry, fish, milk, and nuts are good sources. Growing bones and teeth need calcium: broccoli, almonds, and calcium-enriched juices are good sources. Iron is lost in the menstrual blood flow, so girls need more iron in their diet. Boys need it too, because their blood volume and tissue growth is increasing so much. Iron is found in red meat, peanut butter, apricots, and dark, leafy green vegetables. Zinc is also an important mineral: it is found in chicken, lean meats, dairy products, and whole grains.

C   What are the benefits of healthy activities and snacks?

Alice and Alan point out that a short break for physical activity in the afternoon would increase students' mental alertness. Most teachers and parents agree that vigorous sports and PE programmes help to improve learning ability. Exercise and physical activity reduce stress, boost self-esteem, aid weight control and turn fat into muscle.

Eating a healthy diet leads to more positive energy and fewer mood swings. The 'sugar high' is a reality—students may feel a great uplift from a chocolate bar or fizzy drink, but later on they will 'crash' down and be more exhausted than ever. Healthier snacks result in a more sustained flow of energy throughout the day.

2   Accepting

Guided Work

Activity 1

Ask students to say briefly how they feel after a prolonged period of study—mentally, emotionally, and physically. Then ask them stand up and do some physical exercises—stretches, running in place, touching their toes, deep knee bends. When they have settled down, ask them to say briefly how they feel now—mentally, emotionally, and physically. There should be a big difference.

Point out that physical exercise is refreshing, and helps them overcome boredom, the tendency to slip into temptations, feelings of depression, moodiness, or irritation.

Activity 2

Ask students to answer the questions in Activity 34 in their Books (p.235).

Activity 34

> 1.   Write down your conclusions and opinions of the story.
>
> 2.   Did you notice a change in Alan during the course of the book?
>
> 3.   Do you think you are more likely to succeed in getting special permission from adults if you present your case well and act responsibly?

3   Doing

Evaluation

Activity 1

Point out to the class that the best results come from plenty of physical activity.

Activity 2

Hold a class debate on the questions below, ensuring that students understand the following three levels from the text:
a.   The importance of physical activity.
b.   The importance of good nutrition.
c.   The importance of asking in a courteous manner and for things which are reasonable.

Specific Resolutions

To use exercise, increased physical activities, and healthier snacks to counteract exhaustion, stress, and lack of concentration.

Chapter 34
Mens Sana in Corpore Sano

 General Information

Topic

Health of body brings health of mind.

Content

- Health review for general adolescent care.
- Opposing unhealthy things like drugs.
- False accusations and the real damage they can lead to.
- Appreciating our own growth.

Objectives

Knowing

- Coping with common adolescent conditions such as acne, increased sweat production, etc.
- Understanding how closely bodily and mental health are related.
- Understanding the damage false accusations can do.

Accepting

- Appreciating the changes to be expected in the teenage years.
- Appreciating the importance of truth in relations with others.

Doing

- To exercise, eat and sleep well and so increase mental alertness.
- To respect other people's good name.

Areas of Human Development to be Emphasised

- Looking after oneself.
- Being positive and sincere.

Class Plan

1   Knowing

Motivation
Story context:

The students continue to learn about health from Mr Radigan. A false accusation against Alan is refuted. They look back over the year as the summer.break approaches .

Introduction
Alan is exonerated after a smear campaign links him with drugs. The students learn the close association between physical and mental health, and tips on personal care.

Presentation
Key Ideas

▸   Standing out against unhealthy behaviour is good.

▸   Adolescence is a time of transformation to be viewed optimistically.

Topic Development

A   Health review

Mr Radigan gives a quick review of basic adolescent health care issues:

"But you know that physical exercise produces sweat," he continued, "and of course you're producing more of that now. So it is even more important to shower every morning and use deodorant. That way, when you take exercise you'll be protected from body odour. And, as a bonus, so will your classmates and teachers!"

"And it's not just sweat that your bodies are producing in increasing quantities," he said. "They're also producing more oil. When you were younger, you might have been able to wash your face just once a day, but now you should really wash it in the morning and in the evening with soap and warm water. This will help with the acne too."

"Of course, diet plays a big part in body odour and acne. Some teenagers suffer from acne, and one reason for that is that a high-fat, oily and sugary diet shows up on the face. So you want to be very careful about what you eat. A good, healthy diet means reading labels and finding out what's in foods. If there's something bad on the list, it would be a good idea to avoid that food. You could look and see if the bread products you eat have unbleached flour in them—that's healthier than bleached (or white) flour. And watch out for chemical additives—MSG [monosodium glutamate] for example. They are not good for you, and they accumulate in your body over time."

B   Standing out against unhealthy things like drugs

Alan is known as 'The Rebel' because of his uncompromising attitudes and his readiness to question authority. However, he draws a sensible line about drug use: *"I'm not that much of a rebel... I'm not stupid. I don't want to screw up my mind and body with that stuff."*

Encourage students to use their adolescent rebelliousness against things that are bad for them, like drugs, unhealthy diets, premature sexual relationships, pessimism, etc.

166

C **Conclusion**

The transformation from child to adult, with adolescence as the 'in-between' phase, is momentous. Reread with students Charlie's and Alice's attitudes about growing up and adolescence:

"So much has changed over this year," she said on the way home. "You've changed, I've changed, our friends have changed."

"Hmm. I'm glad it's almost the summer holidays," Charlie said thoughtfully. "At least Year 9 is supposed to be a bit easier."

Charlie hoped that would be true. So much had changed this year, he thought—looking back, Year 8 seemed like an 'in-between' time when they had begun to leave childhood behind but were not yet adults. Still, there was a lot to feel good about, and Charlie was looking forward to the challenges and rewards of becoming a man. There was so much to do, so much to learn, so many people to get to know…

They waved at Alan as he rode past on his bike.

"Charlie, do you think there'll be so much new stuff next year?" Alice asked.

"Yes," he said. "But I'm looking forward to it."

Alice smiled. "No more Peter Pan, then?"

"No," Charlie replied. "Anyway, we're growing up—we can't put the clock back!"

"I like growing up," said Alice gravely.

Alan puns on the word 'high' with youthful exuberance. Youngsters who live healthy and full lives enjoy themselves and can look forward to their futures with every confidence.

2   Accepting

Guided Work

Activity 1

Someone has gone to Never Land and brought back some fairy dust which keeps you at a certain age forever. Ask the students to think at what age they would like to stay, and to write down why.

Activity 2

Do the 'half-full' or 'half-empty' exercise. Fill a large glass half-full with water. Ask the students what they see. Tell them that to see the glass as half-full represents an optimistic attitude. Good things happen to those who expect them!

Encourage them to see their own adolescence as a half-full glass rather than a half-empty one and to enjoy these years fully by discovering their unique gifts, making many good friends, participating in many healthy activities and growing toward a healthy, happy adulthood.

3   Doing

Evaluation

Activity 1

Ask for volunteers to read their short essays aloud or to allow someone else to do so.

Ask students to debate the various ages and reasons that have been chosen. If any have chosen their own age as best, ask them to talk to the class about it.

Activity 2

Evaluate from what has come out of their essays and discussion whether students have a positive or negative or mixed attitude toward their own adolescence. Once again, encourage a positive attitude. Ask if they like or want to be like Alice and Charlie, who are basically healthy and happy. Alan, too, has his admirable side.

Specific Resolution

To take a positive, optimistic, forward-looking view of adolescence and growing up.